Ethical Behaviour in the E-Classroom

CHANDOS
LEARNING AND TEACHING SERIES

Series Editors: Professor Chenicheri Sid Nair and Dr Patricie Mertova
(emails: sid.nair@uwa.edu.au and patricie.mertova@education.ox.ac.uk)

This series of books is aimed at practitioners in the higher education quality arena. This includes academics, managers and leaders involved in higher education quality, as well as those involved in the design and administration of questionnaires, surveys and courses. Designed as a resource to complement the understanding of issues relating to student feedback, books in this series will respond to these issues with practical applications. If you would like a full listing of current and forthcoming titles, please visit our website, www.chandospublishing.com, email wp@woodheadpublishing.com or telephone +44 (0) 1223 399140.

New authors: we are always pleased to receive ideas for new titles; if you would like to write a book for Chandos, please contact Dr Glyn Jones on gjones@chandospublishing.com or telephone+44 (0) 1993 848726.

Bulk orders: some organisations buy a number of copies of our books. If you are interested in doing this, we would be pleased to discuss a discount. Please email wp@woodheadpublishing.com or telephone +44 (0) 1223 499140.

Ethical Behaviour in the E-Classroom

What the online student needs to know

CASSANDRA J. SMITH

CP

CHANDOS
PUBLISHING

Oxford Cambridge New Delhi

Chandos Publishing
Hexagon House
Avenue 4
Station Lane
Witney
Oxford OX28 4BN
UK
Tel: +44 (0) 1993 848726
E-mail: info@chandospublishing.com
www.chandospublishing.com
www.chandospublishingonline.com

Chandos Publishing is an imprint of Woodhead Publishing Limited

Woodhead Publishing Limited
80 High Street
Sawston, Cambridge CB22 3HJ
UK
Tel: +44 (0) 1223 499140
Fax: +44 (0) 1223 832819
www.woodheadpublishing.com

First published in 2012

ISBN: 978-1-84334-689-0 (print)
ISBN: 978-1-78063-306-0 (online)

British Library Cataloguing-in-Publication Data.
A catalogue record for this book is available from the British Library.

Typeset by Domex e-Data Pvt. Ltd.
Printed in the UK and USA.

In loving memory of my grandmother Margaret Goldsby

Thank you God for creating me
Thank you Jesus for not leaving me
Thank you Holy Spirit for guiding me

To my family, friends, and students: thank you for your
unyielding love and educational challenges.

Education implodes the walls of ignorance
C. Smith

Contents

List of figures

Acknowledgements

I would like to thank my global and local contributors to the book who provided quotations and remarks on the diverse topics. Your perspectives reinforced the message of the book – and that is to help those working at a distance to be successful and understand online protocol. I would also like to thank the authors cited in the book who have provided foundational principles about critical thinking, self-directed learning and ethics. These concepts added to my seminal research about critical thinking, self-discipline and ethical theories as they relate to distance education.

I am especially grateful to my publishers, Chandos. It takes a leader in any discipline to have vision and be unique. The staff and editors at Chandos are visionaries and they realize that as technology changes, so must the content and instruction. With their unique books and products, they are a leader in the industry to those who will soon follow.

I am sincerely grateful to my husband. He is my motivation, consistently reminding me of my true self and my limitless possibilities. I would also like to acknowledge my parents, siblings and other family members. A writer can imagine and construct, but is sometimes challenged – that is when family reminds her of her special gifts; you did that for me.

Finally, I want to acknowledge my students. You have improved my leadership, communication, and perceptive skills. You taught me as well.

About the author

Cassandra J. Smith, M.Ed., has been writing for more than 20 years. She started as a journalist for a CBS affiliate in the United States of America and has now written general education courses for distance education programs in higher education. She studied adult learning theories in graduate school and is currently an online instructor. Smith has experience working with novice and experienced adult learners.

Smith has added to the body of literature of online pedagogy. In 2008, she wrote a book called *Who Let this Disaster in My Classroom?* The book contains best practices for worldwide faculty teaching at a distance. Facilitating virtual teams and engaging in discussions in the online environment are some of the highlights of her book. Smith has also trained online faculty on how to facilitate a successful online class.

She has interacted with diverse adult learners, using asynchronous and synchronous types of communication, in her years of online teaching experience.

Smith holds a Bachelor of Science in Communication from the University of Mobile, and a Master of Arts in Education with an emphasis on Adult Education and Distance Learning from the University of Phoenix. Smith is a doctoral PhD candidate in the Postsecondary and Adult Education discipline.

Faculty staff are encouraged to contact the author at *cassiesmith41@gmail.com* for further information, notes and resources.

Introduction to ethical behaviour in the e-classroom

It's late Sunday night. You are alone in your room. You have been running errands all day. You had an argument with your significant other. Your roommate is asking for your share of the rent money, and your check was short two hundred dollars. You have a paper due tomorrow. You are in no mood to write an essay this late. Your planning is out of kilter. You search the Internet and retrieve the results of an essay about your topic. You have a sudden strange feeling as you skim through the essay, thinking to yourself that this is good. It will make for a great paper. But, you know that it is wrong, and only entertain the thought for a split second before writing your own paper. Rewind for a second. You skim through the essay, thinking to yourself that this is good. It will make for a great paper. You say to yourself, "I can change a few words and no one would be the wiser." Rewind for another second. You skim through the essay, thinking to yourself that this is good. It will make for a great paper. You say to yourself, "I can use it, but what if I get caught? The instructor might discover that I didn't write the paper. Is it worth the chance of getting caught?"

Your mind goes round in circles as you wonder if you should use the paper. You comment to yourself, "Should I or should I not go down this dubious path? What shall I do?" The choice of good or bad reverberates in your mind. For some of you, it is not a dilemma of right or wrong. You know that it is not right and will submit your essay by doing the hard work or accept the late points that could be applied if you do not make the deadline. Some of you also know right from wrong, but choose the opposite, which is to cheat with trepidation. Some of you will use the paper with no remorse. Doubtful, decisive, remorseful, noncommittal, resolute, or questionable could all describe parts of the ethical or unethical choices in this scenario or any given ethical scenario. This textbook explains what it means to be ethical in online classes – in higher education. This will be accomplished by addressing ethical and unethical choices and patterns of good and poor behaviour online.

Fortunately, distance education has made it possible for working adults, or adults who desire to continue their education, to obtain their degrees online. Attending classes online means that you have a computer that is Internet ready and connected. You log in on your computer, at a time convenient to you, to your school's electronic software to complete class work and meet assignment deadlines. Your instructor is not aware of who is behind the computer, just like you are not aware of your instructor. You do not know each other's personal traits, profiles, appearances – unless there is a picture of your instructor on the school's website – learning styles, and/or behaviours. You start this task with an attitude of blind trust, hoping to work with an ethical instructor, and the instructor hopes that students will submit their work and make ethical choices. You also do not know who is actually grading your work. The instructor does not know who is submitting the work. Yes, as the student, you are enrolled in the course. Yes, as the instructor, the person is hired to complete a job. But, who is the real you behind the computer? Who is actually doing the work as the student enrolled in the degree program? Is it you or the Internet? Is it family members, peers, a hired person, or chat rooms?

Therein is the dilemma of ethics online. Although some instructors make unethical choices as well, this book will address concerns of students' ethics or lack of ethics in the online classroom. You will read about several true cases of unethical student behaviour in online classes. You will learn what is considered a violation of the code of ethics when pursuing your online degree. You will learn how to avoid issues that will place you in the position of victim or offender while being an online student by reviewing topics such as plagiarism, critical thinking, and communication methods.

This is a book of reflection and examination. It is real, current, and not figurative. Therefore, some of the statements are crude. You will reflect on times when you made good or poor decisions and the results of both. You will examine others' choices and actions and then review the repercussions. You will have the opportunity to decide on your possible course of action for some of the dilemmas presented in this book. You can decide where you are with your moral make-up. If there are any misconceptions or poor thinking patterns that have plagued your life and thought processes, you can develop an ethical plan to be a successful online student. If you are good and feel strong about your convictions, you can still grow and ensure your success as an online student. Throughout this book, you will have the opportunity to reflect on your private thoughts and really self-assess your actions. The first of these is located in Figure I.1.

> ## What would you do?
>
> Would you use the paper from the Internet as explained in the introduction or do your own work? Would you run a red light if you thought no one was watching? Or, do you think that someone is always watching? Does the fact that someone might be watching stop you or influence your ethical views about any situation? A plagiarism study of policies was implemented by Dr. Wendy Sutherland-Smith, of Deakin University in Australia, using six universities representing three different national categories: The Group of 8 (Australia), the Russell Group (United Kingdom), and the Ivy League (United States of America):
>
> "Universities listed in each national category were then compared against the Times Higher Education Supplement (THES) world rankings for the top 200 universities worldwide from 2007 to 2008. All 18 universities in the study have consistently located plagiarism in disciplinary or academic misconduct regulations of university policy provisions."

Figure I.1 Self-reflection

Course design

This course is designed for adult online students:

- new to ethical expectations in electronic learning and class expectations;
- challenged with interacting in the discussions and written assignments online;
- interested in proper protocol in an online classroom;
- seeking to enhance their study and learning skills;

- seeking to enhance their conflict management skills;
- seeking to enhance their critical thinking skills.

Objectives

You will learn how to:

- identify relevant facts and principles involved in making ethical decisions with the contemporary use of technology and education;
- avoid being a victim of cheating online or displaying this behaviour;
- assess personal patterns of behaviour and the origins of traits that could influence the behaviour of you and your peers;
- illustrate critical thinking by applying elements of the critical thinking circle to make ethical decisions;
- compose clear discussion responses using the basics of Bloom's cognitive taxonomy.

You will gain:

- the ability to write clear messages;
- confidence in electronic learning as a viable option for obtaining a degree;
- knowledge about ethical dilemmas that could influence choices;
- skills to avoid plagiarism;
- understanding of critical thinking concepts;
- discernment for making better choices to meet college goals.

Format

- *Chapter 1* basically introduces students to terms and definitions of the three main concepts that will be discussed throughout this textbook. These are ethics, critical thinking, and plagiarism.

- *Chapters 2 through 7* provide an in-depth review of ethics, critical thinking, plagiarism, the dilemmas that result from certain actions, and possible reasons why some behavioural patterns are demonstrated.

- *Chapters 8 through 10* summarize ethics, critical thinking, and plagiarism in the online classroom, and review the importance of meeting ethical expectations in the e-classroom.

- Chapters consist of one or more of the following: discussion questions, activities, student cases, students' perspectives, and examples of real-life ethical and unethical choices students have made in the online classroom. It is hoped by the author that online students will actively engage in their learning using this book, and even evaluate their own ethical progression online, to be successful in distance education.

Assessing behaviour

Abstract: Distance learning is global. Characteristics of the online learner are constantly evolving, from young adults graduating from high school to older adults, after working for 20 years, embarking on a degree to achieve a goal that never was relinquished despite life circumstances. With the different types of students, learning levels, ethical backgrounds, and technical skills, the protocols and academic methods in the electronic classroom must be defined. These include, but are not limited to, transformational language, critical thinking, multicultural education, conflict management, collaborative learning, and work integrity, which are all included in ethical principles. The definitions of ethics and associated terms are discussed. Students are shown what "good behaviour" means and how "moral reasoning" impacts classroom behavior, and are also introduced to what it means to be an autonomous learner in the online classroom, adhering to codes of ethics. The concept of self-directed learning is explored for online students planning, carrying out, and evaluating their own learning experiences. Students encounter real-life dialogue in the electronic classroom and will have the opportunity to respond with their opinions to the student cases by answering discussion questions and participating in activities. The chapter concludes with information about codes of ethics.

Key words: ethics, code of ethics, self-directed learning.

Ethics definition

What are ethics? *Ethics* are defined as the study of the rules of conduct. The word is sometimes used to refer to a set of rules, principles, or ways of thinking that guides behaviour. Ethics are a set of values that you adhere to with regard to determining right from wrong. Ethics indicate the practice of right action and the greater good. In essence, ethics are a set of principles for how you live your life. Ethics include good human conduct or behaviour.

What does "good behaviour" mean?

Good behaviour is doing what is considered morally correct in the present protocol of the situation. Morals are the rules of conduct and ideas based on right or wrong. In higher education, following the school's rules is good, moral behaviour. Good behaviour is conforming to acceptable standards and rules. This could mean doing your class work and not presenting others' work as your own, or not having someone do the work for you when you are the student enrolled in the online class. In the community, good ethical behaviour includes following the laws of society and conforming to societal order. For some people, ethical behaviour is taught in childhood and gradually becomes innate when making choices. Most people learn right and wrong in their homes during their childhood years and from their environment. For example, you or a childhood friend might have known as a child that telling a lie to parents goes with punishment. You or that person might recall a childhood story about how the punishment was memorable for telling that particular lie. Thus, the process of ethical behaviour evolves into adulthood; good then becomes the opposite of bad or poor behaviour because you, or that friend, understand as an adult that poor choices have repercussions.

If you decide to live by certain standards, known as *values*, that you have set for yourself as you develop, ethical choices are not difficult because you are comfortable with your decisions and want to meet your goals honestly as adult learners. Your *moral reasoning*, the thinking process of deciding on what is right or wrong and identifying the dilemma clearly with regard to situations and daily interactions, does not require a long thought process. You innately know what works for you and what type of work ethic you want to contribute to your own success.

Review student case Zachary in Figure 1.1 and reflect on the student's moral reasoning, his work ethic, and any possible experiences or instructor's comments that might have influenced this student's patterns of behaviour.

Moral reasoning can occur when making ethical decisions. It should consist of stating the facts about the issue and reviewing if there is a problem to start with, as you decide on what is best for you in any given scenario. For good or bad, is there a problem with the student's writing in Figure 1.1? To personalize moral reasoning, the student in Figure 1.1, Zachary, should ask, "Is there an issue with my writing?" as opposed to assuming the victim's role in the scenario. What can I do to improve, even if I question a mistake has been made? What good can come from this learning scenario? What is taking priority over the decision? Is it my pride, beliefs, disruptive behaviour, or is good prevailing? These are questions that can be posed in the moral reasoning stages when making decisions and exhibiting actions in the online classroom.

If you were to assess this issue, you might not have placed yourself in this position from the start to apply moral

---

Student Zachary

I submitted my week three assignment. I am trying really hard, and I feel as if you hate me. I am going to take my concerns to my advisor because I feel as if you are being unfair to me in this class.

Instructor Deem

You have plagiarized in this class, and we are in the final week. You have submitted work past the late policy so the assignment is not acceptable at this point – yet you email me and say that I am "unfair." You have to follow the rules in class to meet assignment deadlines and do your work and not use words from the Internet. When you start taking responsibility for your work and not blaming me as the instructor, you might discover that you can learn and do better. As long as you blame others, such as an instructor, you will possibly make the same mistakes. Did you review my comments on how to avoid plagiarism going forward? To send me an email as such is offensive. You are an adult learner, so it might be time for you to take responsibility for your work.

Figure 1.1   Student case Zachary

reasoning. Sometimes it is visceral for people to make ethical and moral decisions. Other times, making good choices is difficult and poor choices are more appealing. For example, perhaps a child *did not* learn the importance of avoiding telling lies to parents and/or teachers. Or, perhaps the child *did* learn but *elected* to continue with unethical behaviour. Suppose what appears as good behaviour to one person is, in fact, poor behaviour to others, especially when a child becomes an adult. A war then starts to break out about right or wrong, ethical or unethical, good or poor behaviour.

Ethics and e-classes

What does waging the war of right or wrong and ethical decisions have to do with distance education courses? As the distance education student in college, you are expected to follow the rules set by the school. The rules could consist of meeting assignment deadlines, interacting with your peers and instructors in a courteous manner, and being responsible for the integrity of your work. Ethical decisions online could consist of you as the student disciplining yourself with regard to time management so that you can submit your original work and not be placed in situations where time has influenced your ethical principles. As a general rule, if you are the student enrolled in the course, it is your responsibility to adhere to ethical standards.

When students seek ways to learn and take responsibility for their learning, they are being self-directed learners. "Self-directed learning is a process of learning in which people take the primary initiative for planning, carrying out, and evaluating their own learning experiences" (Merriam et al., 2007).[1] When students return to school, particularly online, after years of being out of school or as a result of challenges, they are usually ready to commit to being a self-directed learner. Adults have several reasons for why they are in school, have returned to school, and are ready to commit to the journey of obtaining a college degree. Some reasons include divorce, the need for job growth, and a personal goal that was never realized of obtaining a degree. It seems natural for the adult learner to be self-directed, even with the struggles of reaching the point of being self-directed that some students might encounter. Students eventually start to realize that the amount of effort put into their work and commitment will catapult them into being self-directed and ultimately build confidence to meet educational goals. Review carefully what it means to be a self-directed learner.

Planning

Learning requires planning. For adult learners, planning systematically what they want to learn, where they will pursue their educational goals, and when is a good time in their lives to learn, requires progressive steps and is linear in nature. The adult learner is usually one-dimensional about the idea of being in college and has planned accordingly, although he or she might not realize everything that being in school encompasses. When adult learners return to school, timing is usually a major concern. For self-directed adult learners, this could be attending college immediately after high school. For other self-directed adult learners, this could be attending college after 30 years of being in the workforce. Planning to return to school and identifying optimal times to complete class work requires self-directed planning.

Carrying out

Adult learners can become self-directed by carrying out or seeking ways to hone skills. Participating in online tutorials to enhance writing and reading skills is one way adults can carry out self-directed learning. Reviewing the resources available to aid in learning that the school has is another way to carry out self-directed learning. Learning how to effectively navigate computers and word processors by participating in training can help advance computer proficiency for adult learners. Carrying out becomes a way to learn additional skills that the adult student has assessed regarding areas of personal improvement.

Evaluating

It takes discipline to self-monitor, self-manage, and self-motivate. Self-monitoring and self-evaluating essentially mean the adult learners analyze and review their progress and the need for skill development. Self-managing requires discipline to complete assignments and requires the adult to continually seek ways to learn while being self-motivated to discipline himself or herself to complete tasks in the midst of an often busy adult lifestyle. If the adult learner does not have discipline encompassing these three factors, it is difficult to be self-directed in learning and actually notice progress towards meeting educational goals when self-evaluating. Constant evaluations of time management, quality of work being submitted, new perspectives being learned, or former perspectives being altered are all great ways to self-evaluate as you meet college goals and become a self-directed learner.

How does self-directed learning relate to ethics?

When you have the tools required to meet goals, you make better decisions. You can display good characteristics because you understand good practices. You are no longer accepting indoctrinated ways of thinking because you are empowered as an adult learner with knowledge regarding what works for you to be a morally successful, self-directed adult student.

Another key element for being self-directed and ethical is that you have identified patterns of success. The dilemma of poor choices in learning is almost obsolete because you have assessed what is viable for your learning. You also display a quality work ethic and that leads to good choices.

Activity 1.1 Discussion questions

1. Briefly explain your definition of ethics. Then, provide two reasons why ethical behaviour in distance education classrooms is important and why.
2. What role did your ethics play in determining your degree path and returning to school?
3. Explain how self-directed learning can benefit you as an adult learner. Apply any of the three characteristics of a self-directed learner to your response.
4. Discuss a time when you used moral reasoning to make a good or poor choice. What were the questions that you posed to yourself? Explain the process of deciding on what to do.

Code of ethics

A code of ethics is a set of guidelines that governs the rules to be followed for an organization and the behaviour of its members. If you are enrolled in a university, you fall under the jurisdiction of the institution's code of ethics. If you violate the code of ethics by any types of act, then you must accept the repercussions for the violation. Some code of ethics categories consist of the following: (a) faculty behaviour with students, (b) peer-to-peer behaviour, (c) student integrity of class work (d) sexual harassment prevention (e) discrimination in student-to-student and/or faculty-to-student policies.

Usually, the code of ethics is located in the student handbook. The school could also have policies for student behaviour consisting of netiquette rules, plagiarism, and academic research located in the actual classroom.

Netiquette rules consist of acceptable online behaviour. They could include avoiding profanity, being respectful and courteous to other students, avoiding all capital letters because that appears as if you are yelling at the reader, and avoiding derogatory comments about race, religion, and other discriminatory acts in class. Some students use the *discussion forums*, the main classroom areas where students submit responses to questions and where all peers can read them, to vent. It is unnecessary to curse in class, online. It is not ethical behaviour. Review the student cases in Figure 1.2

Zora commented

Family support – My family support regarding returning to school is to quit and help the family...that is what they think I need to do! Is kind of funny when I type it...So not only do I have to work hard to prove myself but also show my family I can meet my goals. If I say I can't, I already know what they are going to say and that is just one word, QUIT!

    That one word (quit) is my support and motivation! I will scream aloud, HELL NO. I WON'T QUIT!

Chase commented

Current events – I am so frustrated with politics. I think that our country could be run by a jackass and his minions...so this is a difficult question for me to answer.

Lena commented

Goal setting – Professor Tyler, I was trying to plan and set goals when my son was arrested for underage drinking. I was very pissed off after I told him NOT TO DRINK OR DRIVE. I became very pissed off with him and had a difficult time goal setting for myself.

Figure 1.2   Student cases Zora, Chase, and Lena

because these situations are often the realities of online learning and could hinder your grades if you use the discussions for venting sessions.

There is a better way, a more effective way to communicate than the students' responses in Figure 1.2, especially if you feel passionate about your statements in the online environment, and you will learn strategies throughout this course.

Plagiarism

The *plagiarism* policy (ways to avoid cheating and how to accurately represent others' work used in your own) should consist of rules governing others' work. An effective plagiarism policy should provide examples or provide a resource for examples on how to *cite* (document) websites and authors' work when you use the material in your assignments. It should clearly mark the outcomes for students who plagiarize. You will learn more about plagiarism and citing sources in this textbook.

The academic research policy should explain plagiarism as well. It should explain types of website to avoid for research, such as Wikipedia for scholarly work, answers.com, and opinionated information that anyone can edit, when researching for essays and class assignments. It should provide information about the school's library and educational journals. The academic research area should also include response guidelines to discussion questions, or there should be an area in class that explains discussion question response expectations. All these fall under a code of ethics and student expectations for in-school behaviour and should be addressed when you enroll in class. It should be part of the literature in the classroom or be an assignment, such as a scavenger hunt, so that you can search for this information. If not, and if you struggle with any of these or have questions regarding how to behave in class, then you should search for the information or ask your instructor about it. Following the code of ethics should not be taken lightly. It is more than a list of rules; it is exhibiting good patterns of behaviour throughout the entire course and your degree program.

Activity 1.2 Internet research

Research the Internet or the school's library for an article on violating the code of ethics in distance education classes. Summarize the article and explain your views on ethical violations.

Activity 1.3 Discussion questions

1. How can the code of ethics be violated online? Explain how the violation can impact a student's academic success.
2. Why are netiquette rules important? How do you think netiquette rules can be violated in distance education classes?
3. Why do you think that it is important to assess your behaviour in school, work, and social settings?

Summary

Ethics are defined as rules of conduct. When you exhibit acceptable practices in society and under governing bodies of instruction, you are delivering patterns of what is considered acceptable, good behaviour. Your moral reasoning can help in the decision-making process and selecting choices

---

What would you do?

Do you think that behavioural rules are needed for online classes? After all, it is online. Is it difficult to persuade adults to follow rules if they are set in their ways? Is it necessary to use offensive language in class to get your point across? Is it necessary to expand your vocabulary as an adult learner with more academic words rather than use vulgarities?

Figure 1.3 Self-reflection

that work in your favour. Following the school's principles, or code of ethics, is a great start in meeting ethical requirements in higher education. In school, it is important to locate information on netiquette rules and academic requirements so that you can comply with and understand expectations. In addition, self-directed learning consists of planning, carrying out, and evaluating learning practices in order to meet goals. Self-directed learning is self-guided behaviour that the adult learner implements in order to be responsible and structured in higher education. Following a combination of these ethical practices can help you, as the adult learner, make good decisions in college.

Note

1.   Reprinted with permission of John Wiley & Sons, Inc.

2

Ethical theories and e-learning

Abstract: Ethics are founded on ethical theories, some dating back to the nineteenth century. Principles, consequences of actions, and patterns of behaviour are encompassed by theories that try to answer these questions. Why do people behave as they do? Is there a reason behind their actions? Do consequences matter and, if so, will that change the choice? Which types of principles guide behaviour? Assessing behaviour origins can reveal inconsistency patterns that might need altering for individuals to effectively achieve the task – to meet the college goal. Not all behaviours and attitudes should, will, or need to be altered for the adult learner. However, they will have a wider perspective to establish what they will accept or reject as ethical behaviour. Ethical theories are explored to stimulate conversations about behaviour patterns. Students review some traditional theories and consider how they apply in the e-classroom, then review scenarios to determine how a different perspective incites an often unique response. When students learn how ethical theories correlate with behaviour, they have a better chance of engaging with others online. Students then personalize ethical theories and determine their views about them and electronic education by completing activities. Ethical theories and moral character are reviewed.

Key words: subjectivism, cultural relativism, utilitarianism, Kantian ethics.

Ethical theories

A review of ethical theories is needed in order to understand possible reasons why people choose one way of living, or certain practices, over another. A review of ethical theories is also needed to introduce different perspectives. Think about the scenario in Chapter 1 about learning good and poor behaviour at home in which the following statement was posed, "Suppose what appears as good behaviour to one person is, in fact, poor behaviour to others, especially when a child becomes an adult." There are several ethical theories that might provide insight into why what appears to one person as a good practice might not be acceptable in society or acceptable for another individual as a good practice. There are theories that explain why individuals exhibit certain patterns of behaviour. In essence, people have reasons why they act the way they do, select what they select, respond how they respond, which might not be comprehensible to others. In that case, the question of what would make some patterns of behaviour ethical or not is left to be answered. The following review will focus on four main theories in ethical relations, as they pertain to contemporary moral issues and issues in e-education, that might provide insight. The theories are as follows: subjectivism, cultural relativism, utilitarianism, and Kantian ethical theories.

Subjectivism

Ethical *subjectivism* is the belief that ethics are simply statements of personal opinions and personal attitudes. Everyone grows up exposed to different views of what is right and wrong and this leads to disagreements about

---

What would you do?

If everyone has his or her opinions on ethics regarding what is right or wrong, then why are rules required?

Figure 2.1   Self-reflection

ethical issues. "Subjectivists believe that ethics are only a matter of personal opinion" (Panza and Potthast, 2010).[1]

For example, your friend says that cheating in class is fine as long as she does not get caught. You say that cheating is wrong. You believe that it is not right for you, regardless of whether you get caught or not. Your friend's view and your view are correct in ethical subjectivism.

Cultural relativism

Ethical *cultural relativism* is the belief that right and wrong are culturally based for individuals. "According to this premise, no one universal ethical standard transcends cultures. Basically in cultural relativism, right or wrong are relative to one's cultural upbringing. No one overarching ethical truth exists." (Panza and Potthast, 2010).[1] Dr. Wendy Sutherland-Smith, of Deakin University in Australia, commented as follows regarding diverse groups working online:

> It can be very difficult for a young, full-time student with excellent broadband coverage and unlimited download capacity who is studying in Australia to even begin to understand the situation for a mature aged student studying online, part-time in a country such as Papua New Guinea, with irregular broadband coverage

and issues such as monsoons and tropical weather that effect [sic] power supplies and therefore effect [sic] the ability to engage online.

Basically, the young student in Australia could view the student in Papua New Guinea as making excuses for missed work when the student explains her issues in class and expects to receive full points when she submits her work. The Australian student might believe that she is right from her perspective that work must be submitted, no matter what the circumstances. The Papua New Guinea student might believe that she is right from her perspective that circumstances allow for assignment delays in the online classroom. From the cultural relativism view, each culture decides on what is ethical behaviour in any given situation.

What would you do?

If everyone has specific cultural beliefs guiding behaviour, how can individuals demonstrating different ethical views unify in an online environment – especially when diverse groups are working together for a common goal such as a degree?

Figure 2.2 Self-reflection

Utilitarianism

Ethical *utilitarianism* is the belief that the consequences of an action are the foundation of ethics:

> To a utilitarian, the choice that offers the greatest benefits to the most people is the choice that is ethically

correct. In essence, this view of ethics falls under consequentialism. Consequentialism focuses on the outcomes or consequences of actions. Consequentialists believe that the source of right or wrong is nothing more than the consequences (results) of actions. (Panza and Potthast, 2010)[1]

For example, an online employee who is a student advisor for a university is conflicted over her enrollment. She is paid based on the number of students that she enrolls. Her enrollment is low and she knows that students can receive additional financial aid if they are not employed and do not report all their personal incomes on the financial aid form. The advisor realizes that more students enrolled in the course will benefit the school, her as the employee, and the students. The utilitarian view will only evaluate this action based on consequences and what benefits the most people. In this example, the advisor informing students not to report all of their income on the financial aid forms will benefit the most people and, from the advisor's action, there could be consequences; this illustrates the utilitarian view.

What would you do?

Do you think that it is acceptable to help the majority of people as opposed to the minority who might be displaced in any given scenario?

Figure 2.3   Self-reflection

Kantian ethics

How you are inclined to interact in the online classroom and what you consider as respectable behaviour when engaging with your peers or adhering to principles when submitting assignments might be two different actions or a different state of mind. Action steps based on inclination or duty form the next ethical theory known as *Kantian* ethics:

> Immanuel Kant is an 18th century philosopher who developed principles about ethics. Kant believed that the principles you live by should be those exhibited by your own practical reason. He believed that two agents that motivate human actions and ethical choices are inclination and duty. Acting from inclination is when you are motivated by what you naturally want to do. Duty is when you are motivated by the principles given by practical reason. (Panza and Potthast, 2010)[1]

In essence, duty is doing something simply because it is the right thing to do. Kant's ethical view is that the principle behind the action illustrates ethical behaviour and moral worth. For example, let us revisit the cheating example. Your friend says that cheating in class is fine as long as she does not get caught. If she was motivated by what she wants to do, and that is to cheat, but will not cheat only because

---

What would you do?

Is it better for you to act out of duty or inclination when making decisions? Is there a significant difference?

Figure 2.4   Self-reflection

she might get caught, then she is acting from inclination and not necessarily out of duty. If she does not perform the action simply because of inclination, she has no moral value from Kant's perspective. To not cheat because she knows that it is wrong demonstrates ethical actions and moral duty. When you can conquer the inclination, respect moral law, and consider the ethical motives behind the action, then you have responded morally from his perspective.

Ethical theories and e-learning

Consider the theories in distance education classes that you have reviewed. Could it possibly be that you have individuals in class exhibiting parts or all of the ethical theories as their personal practices? Some students could have different ways of interacting in class because of cultural beliefs. Some students could have consistent beliefs about supporting the majority perspectives without a strong sense of self. How would this impact learning? Each of these theories has pros and cons and can be argued either way, especially if it leads you to think that something is right when in fact it is not. A theory consists of educated principles based on research to support the principles. Theories are critical in nature because they are debatable, yet provide guidance for the unknown. It is also important to remember that with ethical issues, individuals can and will have different perspectives as noted in the theories. This can impact communication and ways of behaving. One aspect that is not debatable as a theory is following rules. There has to be order – rules to follow even if it appears that you do not have as much freedom as you desire in the present scenario. Rules have to be followed at work, in school, in communities, and overall in life because unethical actions do have consequences.

Activity 2.1 Ethical scenarios

Review the scenarios below and explain your perspectives on each of the ethical theories that are being presented.

Example A

Sadgati is from India, but is now living in America. Her American friend, Jill, proofreads her work and often edits her sentences for her classes. In return, Sadgati is helping Jill with her online multicultural education class. She answers her discussion questions and gives her ideas from an international perspective. What is wrong with both students' actions? What effect does cultural relativism have in this example?

Example B

Barbara is having computer problems, so she goes to the library to complete her discussion questions. She only has ten minutes on the computer because the next customer will need to use it, so she decides to surf the net to generate ideas and then rewords some of the information to quickly answer her three questions and meet her deadline.

From Kant's moral perspective, what is the implication of Barbara's actions? Which, if any, could be for the sake of duty in this scenario?

Example C

Darren has met his attendance requirements for the week by logging on twice to his online class and submitting responses. He decides to log in the following week, and he realizes that he has a zero for a written assignment that he submitted. He never read his emails from his instructor that his grade was pending because his file was invalid and he had to resubmit by a deadline that has now past. He believes that the instructor should grade his work and allow him to resubmit without penalty. His main premise is that he met his requirements logging in and the teacher is unfair and abusing her authority as an instructor.

What impact does the subjectivism perspective have in this ethical dilemma?

Example D

To Instructor Green,

I am a religious Jew. The Jewish holiday, the Passover, begins next week and I will not be able to meet participation requirements. In fact, I have an issue with the attendance expectations during this sacred season. Why should I obtain a zero if I am obligated to the Passover? I feel as if this is religious discrimination for the Jewish students in class.

From the utilitarianism ethical perspective, is there an issue present? Should the attendance policy be amended to accommodate Jewish students? Explain your answers.

Ethical theories and moral character

Do you ever wonder how different your life would be if you harnessed your energy and drive to make good decisions as opposed to poor ones? This might not apply to all of you. You might have harnessed your energy and drive to make good decisions and feel that you are right where you need to be in your life. Moral character consists of your individual qualities of performing good or bad behaviour. If your moral character is one-dimensional, you might not be willing to adapt to change and view some of your practices as unethical if they are, in fact, poor patterns. There might not be any variations in your thinking or willingness to think on different levels about an issue. If your moral character is multi-dimensional, meaning you are willing to assess your behaviour and are receptive to diverse viewpoints, you can improve on your practices and make better decisions. Think about the cultural relativism theory. You might have missed out on knowing a great person as a friend or colleague simply because you judge them from what you have heard or read about their culture. You immediately dismissed their gifts and contributions to your surroundings because you rejected them based on what could be untruths about their cultural behaviour and a lack of understanding about their culture. You demonstrated a one-dimensional moral character.

Or, as explained from the Kantian view perspective, you could act out of duty to be morally accepting of others' differences. If you think that one of your peer's responses often appear to illustrate a brazen attitude, you accept the student's opinions because you realize that he or she might have different experiences that cause him or her to respond boldly in class and make statements that you might not view as acceptable in an open forum.

Another example would be the utilitarianism theory. You assess your moral character as a result of consequences. You are constantly mindful of the consequences of actions and this has formed your moral character. You are basically genetically designed to display good, poor, or both moral characters because the consequences are essentially ingrained in your mind regarding what happens when you do good and what has happened when you make poor choices.

If your moral character is based on the subjectivism theory, you view ethics as your personal opinions and what you feel is appropriate. If you believe that your moral character is based on the ethical subjectivism view – that ethics are simply statements of personal opinion and personal attitudes – your decisions could simply be based on personal beliefs and not necessarily the reality of the situation.

In fact, when you are online, you can be any character that you want. You could make up elaborate stories simply to answer discussion questions and illustrate the good or poor characteristics of any of the theories. But, you must decide if you are being your true self and gaining the most out of your education. Are you using the best of your mind to reflect on the questions being asked in class? Are you experiencing – fully experiencing – the learning experience? Online learning is a great benefit resulting from technology. Essentially, it is up to you to make your mark as a good character in this educational field.

Simply displaying ethical behaviour does not mean that your moral character will change. However, if you are receptive to change and assessing your moral character, you can begin to accept and reject what you deem as appropriate for your life.

The debate about ethics and morals being interchangeable terms could be supported either way. Some scholars would say that ethics are the concerns regarding societal laws, while morals are the concern with personal choices and behaviour. Whether you believe that they are the same terms or different, what is usually conclusive is that good morals and ethics are what should be exhibited and poor morals and unethical patterns should not be exhibited. Your moral character should comprise good actions and the ability to work out when some choice is unethical.

Summary

In this chapter, you learned about four major ethical theories that can influence ethical perspectives in online classes. They

> ## What would you do?
>
> A student comments that ethics are definitely developed from an individual's moral beliefs, which will have a lot to do with a person's upbringing and his or her religion. And if two people with different beliefs and different morals had to make the same decision, there would probably be a different outcome. They would still think about the repercussions before selecting the answer – people are wired that way! Is this a reason to pardon unethical decisions?

Figure 2.5   Self-reflection

are as follows: subjectivism, cultural relativism, utilitarianism, and Kantian ethics. Ethical subjectivism is the belief that ethics are simply statements of personal opinions and personal attitudes. Ethical cultural relativism is the belief that right and wrong are culturally based for individuals. Ethical utilitarianism is the belief that the consequences of an action are the foundation of ethics. Kantian ethics are the belief that the principles that people live by should be those exhibited by their own practical reason. It is important to be mindful of these theories, when interacting with others in online classes, in order to establish a rapport with peers and help communication flow smoothly. Individuals have different backgrounds, experiences, and beliefs that make up their moral characters and these could influence behavioural patterns and expression in classes.

Note

1.   Reprinted with permission of John Wiley & Sons, Inc.

3

Processing thoughts: critical thinking

Abstract: Ethical decisions are influenced by thought processes. If ways of thinking and knowing contain assumptions, biases, or errors, these variables can influence having an accurate thinking process and also learning outcomes. Students in the online environment have many opportunities to assess their thinking patterns, compose responses in the hope that they are diplomatic, and gather and evaluate data. The interaction process alone in the online classroom requires critical thinking, which means implementing logical thought to problem-solve, compose responses, and manage an array of business goals to make decisions. In the online environment, finding work times that are the most productive, composing responses, interacting with instructors and peers, and enjoying relaxation are some areas where critical thinking is needed and are explained in this chapter. Busy adult learners have to understand this concept and what it means to be ethical and apply critical thinking. If they do not, decisions that are unethical in nature can influence all stakeholders in the e-classroom. Students will review how applying or not applying critical thinking influences the above factors and complete activities. This chapter also includes information about the characteristics of critical thinking and concludes with critical thinking scenarios.

Key words: critical thinking, assumptions, inferences.

Critical thinking defined

Your ethical views will often be evoked when you are faced with dilemmas. You might initiate a detailed thought process that allows you to make a decision that you are comfortable with implementing. Your foundation and path of always making good decisions could help you when you have to make significant decisions in your life. The analytical thinking process that you initiate is called *critical thinking*. Critical thinking is a process of gathering and evaluating data to make decisions and solve problems that you encounter.

When you apply a logical thought process, consider the repercussions and possible outcomes, think outside your normal parameters, reflect on past experiences, use forward thinking to devise new ideas, communicate with others, are open-minded about answers, pose questions and give possible answers to yourself, you are thinking critically in one or more forms regarding your issue. Usually, your experiences form your thinking. Your parents' values, your friends' views, or your relationships can influence your thinking and thought processes. That is why it is important to examine your thoughts and patterns of thinking to be effective critical thinkers and remove any biases or opinions that could influence your outcomes and/ or place limitations on your thinking due to familiarity or mindsets that serve as blockages (an obstruction of clear view). Blockages in critical thinking could be certain biases as stated above and experiences that obstruct clear thought. A blockage with regard to returning to school could be the mindset that says people in your age group are too old to learn how to use a computer, including yourself. When thinking critically, you want to avoid blockages in order to make doable decisions.

Critical thinking in e-learning

When you decided on your school choice, you might have exercised critical thinking. You might have exercised critical thinking regarding your degree plan. When you evaluate and research possible choices to make an informed decision, you are usually exercising critical thinking. You might have exercised critical thinking in deciding on your family's role regarding your school return. You might have asked, "Will they be the support system that I need or will I have to go it alone?" Critical thinking allows for a deeper thought process. It includes looking beyond the surface in order to make decisions and think forward about possible opposition and solutions. If my family does not support me, how will I react? Will I still be able to keep myself motivated and meet my personal goals? Perhaps I should devise a plan of action to return to school.

For personal choices such as returning to school, it might not be as difficult to exercise critical thinking. For unfamiliar decisions like actually being enrolled in an online class, it can be challenging to apply critical thinking. Being enrolled in online classes requires critical thinking because you have to think clearly in order to compose messages, answer discussion questions, and interact with peers on a professional and polite level. You have to think critically when deciding on times that are productive for working, such as when your energy levels are high or when there are fewer distractions in your environment, to submit quality work. In Chapter 9, you will review more information about critical thinking, particularly critical thinking and ethics.

Stephen Brookfield, author and professor, defined four characteristics of applying critical thinking: "(a) Identifying and challenging assumptions, (b) Challenging the importance of context, (c) Trying to imagine and explore alternatives, and (d) Reflective skepticism" (Brookfield, 1987).[1] These steps aid in critical thinking. Review the distance education school-choice dilemma regarding the four characteristics and how they factor into decision making in the following text.

Identifying and challenging assumptions

You are new to distance education. You might have heard that degrees online are not valid. You might have heard that you will not learn as much online as you would in a traditional classroom. You might have family members who frown upon this type learning because they all attended Ivy League schools. These are assumptions about distance education. Assumptions can influence critical thinking and will be discussed in detail next. You might find that you are applying critical thinking to research these assumptions to support your distance education choice. In identifying and challenging these assumptions, you might conclude that distance education is worth a try.

Challenging the importance of context

You might be reflective and remember that you are the type learner who prefers face-to-face learning. You comprehend more effectively with the teacher present in the classroom. You have perceived this to be true about yourself and this is what has shaped your learning. These contextual factors influence your hesitancy about online classes. You might make an assumption that the online environment is not for you – but you do not have a choice because it conveniently fits into your schedule and you want your degree.

Trying to imagine and explore alternatives

As you work to dispel any assumptions, you might discover that distance education is an effective, alternative way to learn. You might discover a new way of thinking and learning that actually works. You might hesitantly agree that distance education is the alternative solution for you obtaining a degree as a busy adult as you explore alternatives and weigh your options of traditional versus nontraditional universities.

Reflective skepticism

As a newcomer to distance education, you might decide this is the best option for you regardless of what family or friends might think about this type of learning. You initiate reflective skepticism because you realize that what works for others does not necessarily work for you. You decide on your own path. The reflective skepticism applies to critical thinking when you make decisions. You support your own decisions and thought patterns with your own research.

Note – Be advised that you will work hard in online classes. It is not an easy route to an education. The online student spends a significant amount of time in the classroom, researching, reading, and writing. The advantages are quite significant as well. You develop a strong database of knowledge and intellect. You gain perceptible perspectives in your field because you have researched and essentially become a subject matter expert throughout your college tenure. You can implement theory with practice because you had to by completing the assignments.

Your outcome might not necessarily be what family or friends would decide. It is your own thought process and decisions that hopefully work for you and deliver your desired outcomes.

Critical thinking is a higher level of thinking. It is not accomplished in haste but is not necessarily a drawn-out process in order to be action-oriented in meeting your tasks and goals. For those who do not exercise critical thinking in class, the poor quality of their work often shows. Assignments are submitted in haste. Responses do not illustrate signs of having applied class textbook material to help form an educated opinion. Peer responses are usually one-line statements such as, "I agree" (with what my peer commented undertones) to simply submit a response. Critical thinking can be learned and is often not addressed as important until students are faced with this concept in higher education or some type of educational situation. Critical thinking and ethics will be discussed in more detail in Chapter 9.

Review students' responses below to a discussion question to determine if critical thinking was applied in their answers.

Activity 3.1 Student critical thinking responses

Topic – returning to school

Question: Have you experienced obstacles returning to school, specifically regarding not being sure if distance education is right for you? How does "confidence" in your choice to return to school factor in dealing with any obstacles that you might encounter?

Student response 1

I was also overwhelmed when I started school. I was ready to quit due to my stress.

Student response 2

I was ready to work hard and commit to school. The textbook explained some of the struggles that adult learners experience. Smith (2008) reported that "adults have fear of failure when returning to school" (p. 28). I was not sure if distance education classes were for me, and my confidence was mediocre. I did have a certain level of fear – but I knew that I would remain motivated. I am ready to meet my degree goals.

Student response 3

One of the biggest hurdles I will need to overcome to be successful is properly allocating my time between work and school. I currently work about 50 hours per week. My second largest obstacle that might prevent me from achieving my goal is my inevitable ability to procrastinate. I wait until the last minute to complete school assignments. In addition, I am a television fanatic. I love my favourite television shows. By simply acknowledging these shortfalls, I have already mitigated the vast majority of risks that are my challenges. I have to work my full-time job – but I am allocating time for work and hopefully that will starve my procrastination. Schedules will help me as well.

Student response 4

When I first started taking this class, my first thought was I can't do it. I was not emotionally prepared to start college. I already had a busy schedule and could not imagine adding more work to my tasks. I did not have a problem with confidence because I knew that I could meet my goals. However, I believed the timing was off. The author explained that preconceived ideas about a task can stifle the process if not addressed. My main concern was emotional preparation. Now that I am in class, I have set up a schedule for myself. It seems school is one more task to add to my schedule, and I am finding that it is manageable. Now I have had the chance to experience the online environment, I have met other people with busy schedules similar to mine and they are accomplishing their goals; I can as well.

Student response 5

In my opinion, distance learning requires a lot of discipline. Distance learning is not my number one choice of instruction; however, at this point in time, it fits my working schedule. I am the type of learner who likes examples to be presented to me and face-to-face interaction with an instructor. My confidence in returning to school to continue my education is really strong. I have the confidence to succeed. Although this is not my first preference, the online learning environment works well.

Critical thinking and posing questions

Critical thinking often requires posing questions to yourself or others in order to make decisions. For example, if you had to decide on sending your child to daycare, you might ask yourself these questions. What are some of the benefits of home training versus daycare training? Is it realistic for my child to stay in daycare half a day while my husband and I decide on a flexible schedule? You might ask for your spouse's opinion about daycare. Posing questions and receiving feedback can help you with critical thinking but not necessarily dictate your choice.

Your preconceived notions about a situation can help or hinder you when you apply critical thinking. What are the assumptions or inferences that you have about the situation? Are there any biases present that could factor into your thinking? "Inference is a step of the mind, an intellectual act by which one concludes that something is true in light of something else's being true or seeming to be true" (Paul and Elder, 2006).[2] For example, if an advisor calls you from the school and leaves a voice mail message saying that she wants to discuss financial aid with you, you might infer that there is a problem with your financial aid. That may or may not be true. It could be that the school offers additional resources that can help you. "*Inferences* can be accurate or inaccurate, and an *assumption* is something we take for granted or presuppose" (Paul and Elder, 2006).[2] An assumption is your prior belief about a situation. If you believe that online schools are easier than traditional school, then you have already come to a conclusion, regardless of whether it is accurate or inaccurate.

How do inferences and assumptions factor in critical thinking?

When people make inferences based on their assumptions, they are not necessarily interpreting the truth. They give meaning to situations or others that are not necessarily the reality. This can impede critical thinking unless the thinker examines any inferences and assumptions that he or she might be applying to a situation to make quality decisions. It takes time to develop skills to identify any inferences and the assumptions that lead to patterns of thinking and behaviour. Critical thinking, and removing assumptions and biases in thinking, may not be an easy process.

Activity 3.2 Critical thinking time management

Read the following paragraph and identify where critical thinking might benefit a college student before and after enrolling in college. Where was critical thinking applied or lacking in the scenario? Were there any inferences or assumptions in this scenario? What could have been done differently? Support your answers.

Zoe's time woes

Zoe is experiencing poor time management skills. She enrolled in college, hoping to quickly earn her degree to take care of her daughter. Zoe is a single mother and has worked as a sales clerk for a clothing store for two years. She is now doing more accounting work in the office. She is enrolled in online classes, trying to obtain her Bachelor of Arts degree in merchandise management. Zoe did great in her first term. Now the classes are more geared towards her degree program, she is feeling overwhelmed. She does not understand what could have changed since her first term, when she is still applying the same study strategies. She does admit to working additional hours and having to commute to take her child to cheerleader practice this term. Her last two tests had less than desirable grades. She received a C on one test and a D on the other. Zoe wants to contact her online instructor, but she fears it will be an inconvenience to him. She comments, "I feel more comfortable speaking face to face with instructors than on the telephone." She tells her friend, "I am not sure about these online classes. Where is the help when it's needed?"

Activity 3.3 Critical thinking dialogue

Select one from the following three situations that could possibly occur in online classes. Compose two paragraphs from the topic of your choice and create dialogue explaining how critical thinking can resolve this situation. Decide what questions you will ask to make an informed decision. Discuss and reflect on any possible factors that might influence your decision in dealing with the situation or any opposition. What should be done in order to help defuse the situation? What ideas or key points are of importance in this decision?

- An irate instructor's emails and grade critiques are derogatory.
- A student struggles with poor reading and comprehension skills to complete assignments.
- A dominant peer comments negatively regarding your class work.

Activity 3.4 Discussion questions

1. Discuss your experience with critical thinking. Did critical thinking play a factor in your choice to return to school? Were there situations where critical thinking should have played a factor, but didn't?
2. How might Brookfield's four characteristics apply to distance education courses and critical thinking? Discuss and provide an example of any personal experience that relates to these characteristics and your decision-making process? Or, explain a work or personal story when you applied or should have applied Brookfield's four critical thinking characteristics.
3. What are some blockages (barriers) that might cause you to not think clearly about obtaining your degree?
4. Apply critical thinking to the following scenarios. In three to five sentences, discuss what you would do systematically to solve these problems.

- A. You noticed that a student in your class copies the responses of other students each week. You reported it to the instructor the week that her response was similar to yours, but the instructor seems not to have responded because the student is still cheating. The class is almost complete. How can you logically resolve this issue or use critical thinking to resolve the issue?

- B. You have decided on a career path (field), but are uncertain of a career choice in that field. How can you narrow down your potential job title by applying critical thinking?

- C. You have been enrolled in online classes for over a year, working on obtaining your bachelor degree. Your best friend is in his first term and informs you that he has already cheated in the first few weeks of class. He comments, "It is easy to cheat online." How would you respond to your friend using a critical thinking application?

Summary

Critical thinking is a thought process that involves gathering and evaluating information to make decisions and solve problems that you encounter. It is necessary to apply critical thinking when you are composing responses in class, completing assignments, and managing your time to meet college goals. Stephen Brookfield (1987) defined four characteristics of applying critical thinking when making decisions: (a) identifying and challenging assumptions, (b) challenging the importance of context, (c) trying to imagine and explore alternatives, and (d) reflective skepticism. Being aware of your assumptions and inferences, removing them from your thought processes, or researching the truth of the situation can influence your decision making and help you make better decisions.

> ## What would you do?
>
> Do you think that critical thinking is relevant in college and life, or is it another concept that you might not use during or after college?

Figure 3.1 Self-reflection

Notes

1. Reprinted with permission of John Wiley & Sons, Inc.
2. Paul, R. and Elder, L. *Critical Thinking: Tools for Taking Charge of Your Learning and Your Life, 2nd,* © 2006. Printed and electronically reproduced by permission of Pearson Education, Inc., Upper Saddle River, New Jersey.

4

Rules of conduct: plagiarism

Abstract: Academic integrity is a significant part of the adult learner's college journey. Academic integrity consists of following the rules and the protocol of the organization. For some college students, rules are often ambiguous. In the online environment, being mindful of academic integrity due to the Internet and its vast resources can be problematic for the adult learner. It is important for administrators, staff, faculty, and students to understand this concept. For the online student, plagiarism can occur and that is a violation of academic integrity. Plagiarism can occur in diverse forms in the online environment. Students will review some plagiarism offenses and what it means to plagiarize in academia. They will have the opportunity to determine factors and predicaments that can lead to plagiarism in the electronic classroom and complete activities. Reviewing the ambiguity from the student's perspective regarding plagiarism is also highlighted. Students will obtain information about the importance of citing sources from borrowed works, whether direct quotations or paraphrased information used to support their ideas. This chapter concludes with student plagiarism scenarios.

Key words: plagiarism, citations, paraphrase.

Plagiarism defined

Plagiarism involves the act of using others' work and trying to pass it off as your own original work. Plagiarism can include using someone else's words or ideas in order to submit an assignment or complete a task and involves not properly documenting where the information was obtained. Essentially, plagiarism is stealing another person's work or ideas. It can occur intentionally and unintentionally.

When plagiarism occurs intentionally, the offender is aware that he or she will use an author's work and reproduce it as an original work. As explained in the introduction, the student is up late and notices a paper on the Internet that is exactly what he or she needs. The student decides to download the paper from the Internet and submit it as his or her original work. Individuals who intentionally plagiarize will use words verbatim or *paraphrased* words of another person and document the work as their own.

When plagiarism occurs unintentionally, the offender usually has some documentation in the work from the author that could be cited (documented with a *citation*) incorrectly. There is documentation of the original work present but a few errors. The source can be traced and there is no malicious intent to avoid citing the author's work.

For example, "Lee (2010) commented that adult learners can take preparatory steps to prepare for college." The student might forget to place the information about the author on the reference page, or there might be no quotation marks if this was a direct quotation, or page or paragraph numbers (from a website). This could be considered unintentional plagiarism. Usually, the instructor will notate in the document what was missing and that is the extent of the issue in this case.

Plagiarism in e-learning

Plagiarism can occur in various forms in distance education classes. Students can plagiarize their assignments, plagiarize by allowing other people to do their work, and plagiarize by lying in order to complete assignments. The key to avoiding plagiarism in college is to know how to accurately document a source and understand how to do your own work. Some authors do not mind students or anyone using their work. They simply want credit for their hard work. They do not want someone claiming to be the original author when they are the original author. Plagiarism will be reviewed in detail in Chapter 7. However, the act is as close as fingertips are to a keyboard. For the working adult learner with challenges, plagiarism might be enticing for some of these learners, especially on less-motivated days. Gürcan Ültanır and Emel Ültanır (2010), both professors of education at Mersin University in Turkey, explained factors in student learning:

> The problems of overcoming health issues and providing a high standard of living and especially the solving of problems that arise put a great strain on lifelong educational programs. An adult is motivated to attend an adult education course by their current needs rather than future ones.

When current needs take precedence over future needs and goals, the act of plagiarism can be tempting for some learners. Plagiarizing in college usually results from the following:

- personal challenges
- time management
- uncertainty of how to cite sources
- laziness
- poor writing skills or being uneducated about writing and the assignment.

Plagiarism is not a desirable outcome for instructors or their students. It is disconcerting for some instructors to have to report to a student that he or she has plagiarized. Read the case of Michael in Figure 4.1 and be mindful of plagiarism from the instructor's perspective.

Activity 4.1 Direct quotations

Find two articles in the school's library on a topic of your choice. Select a direct quotation of interest in the article and explain in five to seven sentences why you selected the quotation. Provide the author's name(s), year of publication, article name, and where you retrieved the information in the library. Review Figure 4.2 for an example of this activity.

Hello Michael,

In reading and grading your responses for discussion question three, I am concerned. I did not notice personal examples from you, but more the sort of information that I can read in the textbook. The discussion question explained that you should share an example when time and/or stress management was an issue and what you could have done differently. The to-do list, exercises, and stress control strategies that you referenced in your response for time management are retrieved from the textbook. It is fine to reference these, but your answer should be reflective of your experiences as well. Let me know if you have questions. Too much textbook material is plagiarism, and you want to avoid that offense in college.

Prof. Timms

Figure 4.1   **Student case Michael**

Smith, C. and Smith, D.R. (2010). Adult Learners and Postsecondary Education. Retrieved from *www.coursetech writers.com*.

"Research has identified the barriers adult learners encounter in attaining their postsecondary degrees, seeking professional goals, and navigating technology."

I selected this quotation because I am interested to know what helps an adult learner be successful in his or her career and higher education. I have an idea about some of the barriers because it has taken me a while to return to school. I had a child at an early age and transitioned into several jobs. Now, I am ready to pursue my college degree. I do have a concern about college writing and disciplining myself to complete class work. Hopefully, the article will be helpful.

Figure 4.2 Direct quotations example

Citing sources

Citing sources can be multifaceted. Some students do not understand how to cite a source and plagiarism occurs. Dr. Wendy Sutherland-Smith commented regarding plagiarism and citing sources:

> Some students I've spoken to know what the definition is, and they don't want to commit acts of plagiarism, but they're just not sure how to go about the citation process. I think in many cases, students become so scared of plagiarism in their academic writing, that they cite every sentence they write – just so they are not able to be accused of plagiarism. Where I've seen this happen, it is heartbreaking, because the student is penalised for not applying any of their own thinking to the work!

Your school will probably have a formal citation style that they prefer you to use when documenting sources and setting up your paper for submission in college. These citation styles could be the American Psychological Association (APA) or Modern Language Association (MLA) styles. Some common citations in an essay include citing electronic sources, authors, books, and/or journals. Here are examples of citing sources in APA style, which is most commonly used in academia. The source must be cited in the essay and on a reference page by you as the student writer to avoid plagiarism. Review Figure 4.3 for an example of citation styles.

You can visit your school's library or academic research information area to learn about the preferred documentation style used at your school.

Activity 4.2 Outline

Prepare an outline for the following topic in preparation for an essay and imagine where you would place citations to support your ideas and document them. This should only be an outline, with an educated guess where a source should be documented to support your views and headings. You should decide on the setup of your outline and place the type of source that you might include in this outline.

For example:

Adult development
A. Definition
B. Adult learning theories

    a. Freud's theory (web source)
    b. Bandura's theory (article – school's library)

Examples of citing sources in APA style

Sources with authors

In the body of work, known as in-text citation, place the author's last name and publication date. For example:

(Paul and Elder, 2006, p.23) – include page numbers for direct quotations and paragraph numbers for websites when using direct quotations.

Smith (2009) reported, "Online classes are awesome, bringing together a diverse group of learners" (p.66).

Reference page

Paul, R, and Elder, L. (2006). Critical Thinking. *Tools for Taking Charge of Your Learning and Your Life*. Upper Saddle River: Pearson Prentice Hall.

Smith, C. (2009). Ethical Behaviour in the E-Classroom. United Kingdom: Chandos Publishers.

Electronic sources without authors

Place the group name of the web page in parenthesis for the in-text citation.

Multisensory learning is when the learner processes information by using all of their senses (Childfirst News, 2011).

Reference page

Childfirst News. (2011). Multisensory Learning. Retrieved from *http:multisensory-learning.html*.

Figure 4.3 Citation styles

Activity 4.3 Discussion questions

1. Why is it important to learn how to cite sources properly to avoid plagiarism? What are ways that plagiarism can be avoided in college?

2. Paraphrase this passage. You must maintain the general idea of the passage. You must include the author's name but place the information in your own words.

May I have your strength?
By Cassandra J. Smith

I held her cracked pepper leg. She had a small cyst that my aunt would not allow the doctors to remove. Actually, that was the least of my 91-year-old grandmother's problems. She was on kidney dialysis for years. Most of the patients starting out with her in dialysis had passed – gone on to glory. As I held her foot, I wondered about the experiences that she had seen, the prejudices that she had experienced that I would only thankfully get a glimpse of in my lifetime. I asked her one day about a dilemma that I was facing – and she said it would pass and that I could overcome any challenge. Maybe that is why she endured; because she had the mindset of overcoming and not letting life stifle her. I often imagined that if I had a miniscule of her strength, I could advance cognitively. She survived breast cancer without having to have any chemotherapy or radiation. She survived the death of her son. She endured her obstacles and showed immeasurable strength.

Nowadays, the younger generation has more than my grandmother's era. In my time, we are not restricted to career choices and life opportunities, but only confined in our minds. My grandmother's generation had less, but their minds were wide open to possibilities and less restrained. They could make lemonade out of lemons, literally – meals from leftovers. I miss her. My grandmother and I had nicknames for each other. I would say "hello gran" and she would say "hello Scottie"... which eventually ended up being hey gem and hey cockeye... and we would laugh. She was funny, genuine, and strong. It was a pleasure having her in my life. She is not dead... just not mentally there.

Activity 4.4 Plagiarism scenarios

As stated above, plagiarism will be discussed more throughout this book. However, document your reactions to the following plagiarism offenses. There are five scenarios where students plagiarized in Figure 4.4. Do you notice a recurring theme from the students or any variations of why they plagiarized?

Example 1

Instructor Green

Hi Codi,

Your paper was 80 percent plagiarized. All information retrieved from the Internet or sources should be documented in the essay as well as on the reference page. As the student writer, you must form your own ideas and then use citations sparingly in your papers. It would be in your best interest if you review the resources for essay writing that I have emailed and visit the writing center.

Codi

Instructor Green, I cited my sources on the reference page. How can you say that I plagiarized? Isn't plagiarism the avoidance of any sources? I have documented where I received the information on the reference page and I do not understand.

(continued)

Example 2

Instructor Lot

Hi April,
Your paper was 22 percent plagiarized. All information retrieved from the Internet or sources should be documented in the essay as well as on the reference page.

April

Instructor Lot, I'm not trying to be difficult, but I did the paper to best of my knowledge. I work in the field so this is common knowledge.

Instructor Lot

Hi April, I am curious. Did you review your plagiarism results? I have also attached your paper to this email with some of the website matches from your work. I understand that you could know this material and it could be chance. But, as the instructor, when plagiarism is reported, I have to go by the results.

April

Well, all I can say is this is interesting. I never got any information from the website, but I will leave it alone, because I don't have the stamina to debate it, but I wish you knew…

Example 3

Instructor Zurich

Hi Tuddie,

Your paper was 42 percent plagiarized. All information retrieved from the Internet or sources should be documented in the essay as well as on the reference page.

Figure 4.4 Plagiarism scenarios *(continued)*

Tuddie

Instructor Zurich, I do not know what you are talking about that I plagiarized. You are not telling the truth. I gave you the reference where the information came from and you are not being fair. I am going to look for another college.

Example 4

Instructor Williams

Hi Tami,

Your paper was 62 percent plagiarized. All information retrieved from the Internet or sources should be documented in the essay as well as on the reference page.

Tami

Instructor Williams, I do not understand why you say that I plagiarized this assignment. This is my work saved on my USB stick from a previous course. So please explain to me how I stole something that is mine!!

Instructor Williams

Did you read the results because this isn't something I made up or I like to occur in my class? I provided feedback about what you did incorrectly. Please explain using information from the Internet because I don't know anything about your USB drive or how you equate this to plagiarizing. Are you saying the plagiarism detection software is incorrect? Are you saying that you wrote a paper in another course, was graded, and used the same paper in this class? If so, that is considered a recycled paper and it is plagiarized, regardless of whether you wrote it, because it was already submitted and graded in another class.

Tami

So in other words I have to rewrite it and submit it again... I did not steal someone else's work.

(continued)

Example 5

Instructor Swift

Hi Terry,

Your paper was 37 percent plagiarized. All information retrieved from the Internet or sources should be documented in the essay as well as on the reference page.

Terry

Instructor Swift, I understand what I have done......this class has given me problems since the beginning. I truly want to write correctly. It is so hard for me to find the right words and to format my paper right. I struggle with this every day and want to improve my writing skills. I have read the text and tried to apply writing strategies to my work. I really want to pass this course. Can you help?

Instructor Swift

Terry, I am glad that you have recognized this offense. Visit me in office hours so that we can devise a writing plan to help you going forward.

Figure 4.4 Plagiarism scenarios

Summary

Plagiarism involves the act of using others' work and trying to pass it off as your own original work. Essentially, plagiarism is stealing another person's work or ideas. It can occur intentionally and unintentionally. Students should know how to document their sources and that is called placing a citation in their work. When you understand how to cite sources and when you paraphrase information and cite the source, these steps help reduce plagiarism. Students should complete their own work in class and keep a record of sources to avoid plagiarism. When writing essays and citing sources, you should put the citation in the essay and on the reference page to avoid plagiarism.

What would you do?

Do you think that every website on the Internet can be detected if the school has plagiarism detection software? What are the chances of getting caught cheating online? Is it worth the chance? What do you think cheating looks like on a transcript?

Figure 4.5 Self-reflection

5

Moral dilemmas online

Abstract: Moral dilemmas are ethical quandaries that present challenges as to which decision to make at any given moment. For the electronic classroom, the moral dilemma could very well involve other students. Having uncompromising values, being mindful of the reasons for meeting the goal, and eliminating some of the excuses that could stifle the goal process are ideal strategies to reduce moral dilemmas. Students are introduced to the concept of self-efficacy, which includes having a sense of the variables and decisions that they can control in their lives. If there is a strong sense of self-efficacy, moral dilemmas in the electronic classroom will not be a huge factor. If there is a wavering or poor disposition of self-efficacy, moral dilemmas can be overwhelming. Students will assess moral dilemmas that could occur in the online environment and decide on possible actions due to their sense of self-efficacy by completing activities. This chapter concludes with a review of students' perspectives about ethics, moral dilemmas, and reasons for missed work (excuses) in the online classroom.

Key words: moral dilemmas, self-efficacy, online excuses.

Moral dilemmas

Moral dilemmas can often be controversial and evoke various thoughts and actions regarding particular topics. As an online student, you might find that you are inadvertently in a moral dilemma. In this chapter, there is an extensive list of issues that could occur online. You should know that online classes are viable. If you are enrolled in an accredited college, then there is probably a protocol in place at the school in the event that these issues occur. Therefore, there is no need to be alarmed. However, you should be aware of how you would handle the issue as well as implement some of the strategies at the end of this unit.

Moral dilemmas could be any of, but not limited to, the following issues of:

- having too little financial aid for school and searching for ways to increase the aid that might not apply to you;

- deciding if you want to plagiarize to complete an assignment;

- reporting another student for copying your work;

- reporting an instructor with poor grading abilities;

- reporting an instructor for having too little interaction with the class;

- receiving derogatory comments from peers or instructors;

- seeing racial remarks posted in a peer's response;

- passing information or copying class content for a friend taking the online class, which is a violation of ownership of the instructional content because the content belongs to the school;

- experiencing online conflict with peers or harassment;

- seeing peers who do not show effort in their work such that you feel the need to make negative remarks;

- noticing favouritism for male students by male or female instructors or vice versa;

- enduring venting sessions from students about personal issues as opposed to answering the discussion questions.

If you have issues with other students, you can politely address the student. If that does not work, you can report the student to your instructor. If you encounter an unfair instructor – and it is clear that the instructor might be targeting you – then you can report this to your advisor. He or she should know the instructor's department chair contact information. Keep in mind that most online classes are monitored by other administrators or the supervisors of the instructor, so serious instructor-to-student issues are rare online. Compromising your degree for shortcuts and lying on school and financial aid applications are never advisable actions.

Activity 5.1 Discussion questions

Should there be some type of distance between your initial thought or emotional reaction to some of these issues and any action? In order to better evaluate the truth and gain an entire perspective of the issue, it would be wise to apply critical thinking before reacting. Select two of the moral dilemma issues and decide how you would react initially, then after applying critical thinking.

Self-efficacy

Self-efficacy is your personal belief regarding how capable you are of exercising control over events in your life. This could include completing your responsibilities or illustrating certain behaviours in the moral dilemmas referenced in this chapter. Self-efficacy is your ability to monitor your attitudes and implement certain abilities to be morally suited for a situation. Self-efficacy in online classes could consist of the belief that you are motivated to meet your college goals, no matter what obstacles you encounter. You have the discipline and the belief that you are capable of understanding the electronic software, content, and instruction because you believe in yourself and know that you can seek help, if needed. You have the level of confidence and self-esteem that transcends obstacles.

Activity 5.2 Discussion questions

How would you end the following sentences in a dispute with an online peer or a curt response sent from your instructor? You can create the scenario based on your self-efficacy. These statements are only to get you started:

- If I were wrong to spread derogatory comments about you as my peer, I would apologize.
- I apologize for my behaviour in class.
- I think your behaviour is unacceptable for a college student.
- If it were me, I would take an introductory writing course.

Activity 5.3 Ethics and online moral dilemmas

Review the following examples from online students about ethics online and moral dilemmas. Select one and discuss your views, how you would handle the situation, or express any comments that could rebut or address the issue.

Response one

When students violate the student code of academic integrity, this violation encompasses several areas, such as plagiarism, copyright infringement, unauthorized assistance, and fabrication. If the student writes a paper and uses the thoughts or words of another, without giving proper credit, it is unethical. Or, if the student invents information of any kind, this is not ethical. When a work is acquired without legal permission, this too is unethical. Lastly, when one obtains assistance from another individual who has not been authorized by faculty, this can be a moral dilemma. Each of these examples can spill negatively into the professional arena. If the student is a slacker in school, he or she will be a slacker in the workforce.

Response two

Ethical behaviour is always necessary, but there are professions where ethical behaviour seems to be more necessary. For instance, how many people would choose a doctor where it was known the doctor did not do his or her own work during class or during residency? The same applies to school: who wants to hire an incompetent student who cheated his or her way through school? The moral dilemma would not exist if the student did not place himself or herself in that situation.

Response three

There are many incidents in the news today that reflect how poor ethical behaviour is negatively impacting individuals' careers. I often wonder whether the person had morals to begin with or did other factors as an adult, or experiences, make the person this way. Can situations make people immoral or is the onus still on the person?

Students' unpreparedness issues

Another issue that presents moral dilemmas for students is not being prepared for college. For adults, they can enroll in school and have all the paperwork in order. But time management and commitment to class work can present issues. As explained in Chapter 1, the self-directed patterns of learning and behaviour are not fully developed. The work might be too demanding; issues with children, computers, and/or finances could immediately take precedence over school work. This quandary can result in not dropping the class because that could be costly. Instead, the student decides to plagiarize some assignments to help make it through the challenging times as opposed to committing to the work and doing it, regardless of whether it means waking up earlier, working during lunch time, or allocating time for school in an already packed schedule full of sacrifices.

Waiting for responses from instructors can present challenges online. The lag time for emails can be taxing for students when they want an immediate answer. Therefore, students can turn to the Internet for the answer or copy someone else's work as a model in class. The student's schedule does not include the time to wait for an instructor's response and that can be a recipe for disaster.

Would you succumb to cheating if you were frustrated and wanted an immediate answer from the instructor? If you were presented with a scenario or lesson that you did not comprehend, even after the instructor responded to your question, would you search the Internet and copy the answer or format to meet your assignment requirements? Would you assume that the instructor probably thinks you understand, based on his or her feedback, and you do not want to keep emailing? These are moral dilemmas that can occur online, and you have to be ready by defining or knowing the type of moral character that you exhibit in any given moral dilemma.

There is a range of issues that the adult learner could be presented with and have in online classes. In essence, your ethical behaviour and your morals can truly impact on completing your degree program or having to restart a program. Sometimes, it is not an ethical choice but unexpected events, such as health challenges, that could hinder the degree process. The good news is that the online classes are still there, available for the adult learner to refocus and get back on track. The scope of the issues that have been commented on by online students includes:

- being incarcerated for various reasons;
- driving under the influence arrest;
- spousal abuse;
- children issues;
- lacking finances for a working computer;
- living in rural areas with minimum computer access.

Online excuses

Sometimes, issues are well known by students before enrolling in the class, such as not having a working computer, and they enroll in spite of challenges. The onus is still on the student because it is a personal degree choice. In essence, it is your responsibility as the student to meet your degree goals. That entails having a working computer online, completing assignments, interacting in class as scheduled, and basically following the rules if you want the degree.

How much information do you think that you should disclose to your instructor about your issues? Are you mindful that the instructor is human with issues as well? Read the student case in Figure 5.1 and then respond.

Excuses can be truthful and also can be loaded with exaggerations. Falsifications or untruths for work problems to be pardoned are often composed to evoke sympathy from

Hello Instructor Ronson,

I have some questions and a few statements for you. To be honest, I am dreading this class. I really don't know that much about technology. In fact, I just learned spell check during my last class because I had significant spelling errors in my discussion posts. I don't even have a cell phone or digital camera. So I am feeling extremely incompetent. I also don't know how to use Microsoft Word or any of the other programs required for this class. I am on social security disability with three children. I also wanted to let you know that I was in a car accident and as a result suffered a traumatic brain injury. I have severe memory issues. It is difficult for me to say or write words and express myself. Can you help me? I want to do great in class. Thank you. Steve

Figure 5.1   Student case Steve

the instructor. Remember your responsibility as the student and you will be fine. Review more excuses from online students to instructors regarding missed work or late submissions:

- I cannot find any business professionals to interview for my project. Can you help find someone for me?
- Family issues have burdened me this week. My sister had surgery and I had to take her. My assignment is late.
- My dog jumped on my keyboard and my work is gone.
- I am not going to answer this question as stated because it is against my religious belief.
- My Internet isn't working.
- I have two kids to take care of.
- I have been sick for days.

- I do not have Internet access and I am on vacation. I will submit my work when I get back from Hawaii.

- My husband and I have been arguing all week.

- My children are in town. May I have two weeks to submit my work?

Summary

Moral dilemmas can occur online. They range from students' lack of preparation for school to students' comments and actions in class. You could be in a moral dilemma or observe them occurring in class. As an online student, you should know how you would respond to diverse issues online and have a good sense of self-efficacy. Self-efficacy is your personal belief regarding how capable you are of exercising control over events in your life. Online classes are not psychological centers but a place for learning. Your instructor is there to facilitate the class, not to solve your personal problems or read excuses for missed or late assignments. It is your responsibility to do your work and avoid excuses.

What would you do?

Do you think that you could reason your way out of a moral dilemma to make a poor choice and justify it, such as using a paper that has been graded in another course as an original work for a new class? Do you have sharp skills such as these to trick the instructor?

Figure 5.2   Self-reflection

6

Transformative language: communication in e-learning

Abstract: Electronic communication, the language, tones, and word usage, can be curt and impersonal. When communicating heavily by correspondence, misinterpreted or unintentional emails might result in conflict. In addition, individuals exhibiting introversion, extraversion, sensing, or other types of personality trait, impact group dynamics and engagement. Online classes are the instructional strategy for transforming written communication. Text messages, emails, and instant messages are not the most formal ways of communication in the technical era. The abbreviated responses and shortcuts to communication have an impact on academic and formal writing. This chapter explains the importance of students transforming their language to a more professional and academic quality, and has activities for students to engage in to transform their communication styles. Conflict styles are also introduced that usually manifest as a result of miscommunication. Students will review information about multicultural education in the online classroom. This chapter concludes with information about individual personality styles, providing insight into ethical behaviour.

Key words: transformative communication, conflict resolution, personality styles.

Transformative language

Since the pervasive usage of technology, communication (delivering and receiving messages) is accomplished through correspondence. In essence, you communicate online through written messages and send a lot of emails to instructors, form responses to peers, and chat with fellow classmates, all in writing. There is a mode of delivery that is acceptable when communicating through correspondence in distance education classes; that mode is professional. Communication should be professional because you are part of academia. Even though you might be in diverse working locations, such as in your home, office, or even on your cellular phone typing a message for an assignment, you still have to remain professional in your e-classes. It is part of your ethical duty as a college student to ensure that integrity is upheld when communicating. You have to consider the recipients. Who will receive this message? You have to consider the unintended. Who might read this message that you did not anticipate, such as another school administrator?

Transforming language

How do you transform your language from jargon to scholarly? How do you transform your language from curt to clear? How do you avoid swear words in a professional setting? *Transformative* language occurs when you begin communicating professionally when you are accustomed to communicating casually. Communication should consist of sending and receiving clear messages. As a communicator, you want to send an effective, comprehensible message. You want to hear and comprehend the other person's message so resolution steps can be implemented in any given scenario, but that will not happen when messages are misunderstood. Transformative language requires you to think differently and respond differently. It requires you to be receptive to learning new ideas, to review scholarly literature, and replace old and often ineffective types of speech. In essence, you are replacing poor patterns of communication with good patterns of communication. This requires a lot of effort from an adult learner. Some transformative communication strategies could consist of, but are not limited to, the following:

- Being receptive to feedback from instructors – this is not always easy for adult learners. In an open forum, in the discussion area, in class, or individually in assignments, some adult students might feel intimidated by another adult professional explaining how to improve on their weak areas. College is a learning time, but that does not necessarily mean that adults are willing to accept the feedback or feel that it is warranted.

- Researching a scholarly writer and reading his or her material.

- Looking up alternative words to avoid jargon.

- Listening to educational CDs or audio books to understand correct word pronunciation.

- Keeping a journal of new words and using them in a sentence frequently to aid in recall.

- Practicing writing complete sentences and speaking correctly as opposed to in fragmented statements. For example, "going to lunch everyone" when it should be stated, "I am going to lunch." "Bring me that mail" when it should be stated, "Please bring me the mail."

Instead of viewing the online classes as a place to relax and chat, you have to be mindful of higher education in this new form and that it is a professional environment. Instead of typing that you are *pissed off,* you should type *I was upset when this occurred* but explain the positive or how you are getting beyond a challenge. Remember, school is a positive step. Having a degree is a positive stride. Assert the positive attributes of this time in your life.

You have to replace the information that is not working in your favour with quality information. That is how you are transformed into a more proficient communicator, both verbally and in writing.

Read the following messages and record your thoughts about each occurrence.

Activity 6.1 Email communication

Liz email

My name is Liz. Years ago, I responded to an insult in an email from a colleague. It was what is considered a "flaming" email. Have you heard of this type of message? Either you or someone else sends a hostile, intimating, or insulting message. One of my colleagues sent me a message, so I responded with a flaming email. It was childish, but I did it at the time. My supervisor told me to always call someone. We were friends so she felt comfortable sharing this information with me because that way the flamed email is not in writing. Emails are permanent.

Questions

What do you think about flaming emails, or emails in general, with this new-age communication, knowing that your words are, in essence, forever retrievable? What are your ethical views on sending emails? What did you learn from the Liz story, or do you have any thoughts to share?

Trent email

My name is Trent. I have a question for my instructor. If the message is not what the receiver wants to hear, can the email be perceived as derogatory, regardless of whether that is not the intent?

Instructor's comment

If the message is not what the receiver wants to read, the message could be perceived as negative. What can help is beginning with a greeting, appearing sympathetic regarding the issue, and considering the word choice. But, even if the unappealing message is placed in the middle or at the end of the email, it would not change the actual message. Messages should be clear. You do not want the reader to misinterpret the importance of the message, regardless of whether it is a good message or not. Remember, there is always the telephone or another appropriate way to communicate if this is a major concern.

Questions

What are your thoughts on the Trent scenario and the instructor's feedback? Have you encountered misinterpreted communication through email? How do you think that you can overcome some of these issues in writing?

Alex email

My name is Alex. I sent the following email to my online instructor:

Hello Instructor Grey, I am one of your students and I am writing because I have not received quality feedback from the assistant regarding my written assignments. I do believe that this assistant is uneducated. When I ask questions, it is as if I am taking a trip to Idiot Island. Would you please intervene? How long do I have to wait for substantive feedback on my draft so that I can know what is expected for my final paper?

Instructor Grey

Hi Alex,

I have spoken with the assistant and she is copied in on this email, and I forwarded your original. She also has documented responses to you. Did you check your spam folder? In addition, I have read the feedback and it is substantive. I would like to be copied in on all correspondence from now on from both of you.

Questions

What are your thoughts on the Alex scenario? Were the instructor's actions acceptable when she copied the assistant in on Alex's original email and the instructor's response? Please explain.

Activity 6.2 Jann's response

How can the class discussion response in Figure 6.1, that is more similar to a casual text message with significant spelling and grammar errors, be transformed into scholarly words?

Hey Jann,

I like ur response. I was plz to know that you are binschool and struggle with writing. Grammar it is very important in a written document. "Because" the frist step in any piece of writing is to determine its purpose. So any written document, sentence, clauses, etc. by using these correctiy, it will help the reader not get side track, it will help your reader understand your writing.

Figure 6.1 **Student case Jann**

Online tone

Messages can carry a tone. Certain words or phrases can appear to be harsh, even if that is not the intent. Some of the challenges of communicating in writing include the absence of facial and verbal expressions and body language. Therefore, if a person is having a bad day or if the wording is in the wrong form for the receiver, the tone of the email can be negative, even if that was not the original intent or it was not a deliberate personal attack on the receiver. Review the following message in Figure 6.2, which is an example of a student's response to her peer. The topic was about changes, goal setting, and returning to school as an adult learner. Notice the sympathetic statements in the first response and the unsympathetic statements in the second student's response regarding the same issue.

Online tone is not an easy skill to hone in messages. Words can be perceived a number of ways online from what was intended. If you are a sensitive person or a person who likes to joke, this might come across incorrectly online in messages or affect the way you read a message from someone. Your personality traits might not be displayed in all messages correctly. You have to be mindful that you want your messages to be as accurate as possible and remember that you are interacting with diverse students and instructors. Consider the simple statements that can be reworded to avoid unwarranted feedback and conflict from your peers.

Examples:

- *Original*: "Yeah, right. I do not believe that happened to you."
- *Rephrase*: "That is interesting! I am amazed that occurred."
- *Original*: "Men tend to do that."
- *Rephrase*: "Some males display these characteristics."

Hi Professor and fellow students, this is Lynn,

I had set a goal for having kids and going to college in my twenties. I thought I had planned everything out so well but an unforeseen problem occurred. I had planned and saved money – all of which were part of my goal so that I could finance my education. The part I didn't plan on was my husband being hit by a drunk driver. He survived the accident, but we later found out he had traumatic brain injuries. I couldn't believe this was happening. I wondered what this meant for my future. I realized that I could plan but I had no control over what my life would consist of in the future or even the next hour. I started to understand that planning isn't all what it is cracked up to be and that setbacks are inevitable. My husband is still alive and is considered disabled. I no longer try to set goals because I know that I have to take it one day at a time.

Hi Lynn,

This is San. I am sorry about your challenges. Believe it or not, my husband also suffers from brain issues because he was also hit by a drunk driver – thrown 35 feet in the air and landed 10 feet away on his head. I see what he goes through every day. So I know what you are going through as well. Think of it like this, God has a plan for you or you wouldn't be here today. I still make goals just in case they turn out the way I desired.

Hi Lynn,

This is Angie. I think that you should be grateful that your husband is living. A good man is hard to find, disabled or not. Besides, what does this have to do with goal setting? A goal is established regardless if it occurs or not...isn't the purpose of a goal to have a plan? Plans are part of life. Everyone knows that we really have no control so might as well try; it cannot hurt anything as opposed to being bitter.

Figure 6.2 Student case Lynn

- *Original*: "You are delusional. I honestly would never do that."

- *Rephrase*: "I couldn't imagine experiencing that. I have another perspective."

Ethical dilemmas in communication

Communication is a progressive area. It takes years to learn to write and speak effectively. Communicating in writing, communicating with diverse groups, and communicating during conflict can certainly benefit the adult learner and cause growth in this area. What ethical dilemmas could written communication present in the online environment? The information below might be helpful!

Multicultural communication – communicating with peers

In online classes, you will work with a diverse group of individuals. They have multiple demographics such as race, age, experiences, personalities, and religious beliefs. It is your duty as an online, adult professional to be respectful to your peers and instructors. Multicultural classification consists of different ethnic groups. The correct identities for general groups could consist of the following or more ethnic groups: African American or black, Asian, Indian or Native American, Latino/Latina or Hispanic, and white or Caucasian.

You should not have to distinguish groups in class, but if you are in a class where cultural differences or ethnic groups are the subject, you want to be correct in using specific terms to identify races. You do not want to be racial in your responses because this could present ethical dilemmas. Try to avoid placing yourself in the predicament where you are insulting another person's racial background and experiences with hurtful or stereotypical words.

Being mindful that you are participating with a diverse group of students online will help you as you compose your messages. The netiquette rules do serve as a guide as explained in Chapter 1. However, there is much more to communicating online through correspondence. You must apply critical thinking to your responses. Ask yourself, would your statements offend you, let alone someone else? Make your statements personal so that you will know that you do not want to offend someone. A simple statement can be escalated into conflict when you are responding to the discussion questions. Remember that each group and individual have a reason for the type of responses composed and consider the ethical theories and perspectives of individuals when you compose messages. Students derive information from personal experiences in their homes, families, communities, and cultures that constitute their knowledge and guide their behaviour. You can reflect on your own experiences to realize the extent to which remarks will be hurtful or unwarranted.

Typical comments to be avoided to peers include the following:

- Your response does not make sense.
- I disagree with your statements. (If you simply share your experiences and your differences, you really do not have to type you "disagree.")
- Your writing is horrible, and you might want to do a spell check.
- Your racial group tends to display those characteristics.

Communicating with instructors

With regard to the practices that you adhere to with your peers, you must apply these to your instructors as well. They are adults, and you are an adult. Hopefully, each relationship established online will reciprocate respect. If you feel as if your instructor is offending you, address the issue in a polite way. But know that there is a difference between disrespect and instruction. If the instructor is commenting on how you can improve your expression or class assignments, then that is instruction. If you receive point deductions and it is explained in your feedback, then that is instruction – this is not the time for you to argue with your instructor or resort to derogatory comments. Start to assess where you might have not completed the assignment fully, not met objectives, or simply need to grow in that area for a particular part of the assignment. Not obtaining the grade that you desire could mean that you missed completing the objectives. Be mindful that you are in college to learn. If you are not and want to debate with the instructor each time you do not get what you want, then that is childlike behaviour. It is your implicit right as a student to question if you have any concerns. You can ask for more feedback but be sure that you are meeting the requirements and your instructor did not make a mistake. Remember, instructors are human and have feelings as well. There is a level of respect that should be applied. Your instructor has attended college and has advanced his or her degree. You are enrolled in the class to pursue your degree so accept the instruction and guidance. It will make your life easier as an online student. If you cannot resolve an issue with your instructor, contact your advisor to see what your options are for grade appeals and instructor conflict.

Typical comments that should be avoided to your instructor:

- You are stupid.

- I question your grading. (Grade disputes could have a process so be sure to check with your advisor. In addition, assignments sometimes have a grading scale called an assignment rubric that you can review before you submit your assignment. That way, you will know what is expected and won't be surprised with your grade if you did not meet all the requirements. Ask your instructor about this grading scale or the requirements before you submit your work if there is any ambiguity about what to do.)

- Your opinion about me does not matter, teacher, or you know nothing.

Conflict resolution

When you are in *conflict*, do you assess what you are conflicted about – the issue or what is the root of the issue? Sometimes, it is difficult to pinpoint the basis of a dispute. Are you upset because a peer commented about your work or because you presented poor-quality work? Allowing yourself to revisit the cause or foundations of the issue can help resolve conflict.

Changing your perspective about the issue can help resolve conflict. You do not necessarily have to express how you feel about the issue in strong words. You can politely express your concerns and get your point across. There is a difference in a statement that begins with, "You are wrong about..." as opposed to, "I am concerned about..." or "I am so angry about..." as opposed to, "I am disappointed about..." The answer to conflict is sometimes in the wording and how you respond in writing, online. Sometimes, there are students online who will comment about your work and do not have their own work in order. They take it upon themselves to play the teacher role. Recognize these types of students and do not let them incite flaming messages from you. Review the case in Figure 6.3 and comment on how you would respond.

The issue with conflict online in the discussion forums is that some students do not know how to interact with peers. Answering the discussion question themselves is not as difficult a task as interacting with peers. The task for some students involves responding to peers, which is often a requirement online for participation in the discussions. Remember, the main classroom is usually where you will answer the discussion questions online and engage with your peers. Some students feel that other students do not submit quality responses so they feel that searching the Internet for an answer is more desirable to meet requirements. This is not

---

Fraz

Your non-directional hypothesis sounds incorrect because you seem to imply in it that the new reading program will significantly help increase reading. Your interview questions are broad as well regarding this topic.

Alley

You didn't even answer your interview questions correctly last week because the instructor commented that you were off topic – and you have the audacity to comment about mine. Perhaps you should spend more time critiquing your own work as opposed to others....more critical thinking and less judgment of others' work. Aren't we in class to learn?

Figure 6.3   Student case Fraz

illustrating ethical behaviour in the discussions. Here are some tips to help with answering in the discussions when engaging with your peers – you will also learn more strategies in Chapter 7 regarding discussion question expectations:

- Look for similar experiences that you have encountered and expand on those.

- Read about the topic of the week and, of course, the required chapters each week to help build dialogue in the discussions.

- Introduce a new source for the topic that you have researched online to generate responses from students and have them visit the website. Remember, you are not passing the work off as yours, but saying where you retrieved the information and adding to the topic with your peers to advance the discussions.

- Reflect on the jobs that you have experienced in your life to share stories.

- Share where you have grown in knowledge or your challenges with the topic.

- Explain the differences that you have encountered in the students' responses from your own experiences.

If you focus on the content and not on a student's delivery, engaging in the discussions will work in your favour. If you are looking to contradict a person's experience when he or she has experienced it, engaging in the discussions will *not* work in your favour. Remember, you might have encountered the same experiences with different results. This is because people have different perspectives and outcomes that will shape their responses and life stories. If you share your experiences and allow your peers to share their experiences, the discussions will flow.

Following the strategies above is not an ironclad plan for preventing conflicts occurring, but it can help reduce conflict. Conflict is inevitable and often unpleasant for individuals. When you do consider your personal styles, issues, and perspectives relating to others, communication becomes more fluid because you can gain an acceptable tolerance of others' differences as opposed to an immediate rejection of others' differences. You tend to understand human frailty because you recognize it in yourself.

One preferred conflict management method, from the *Thomas–Kilmann Conflict Mode Instrument* (Thomas and Kilmann, 2007),[1] suggests that individuals are inclined to using one of the following five conflict styles: *avoidance* (which involves not discussing the pressing issue), *accommodation* (giving in to the issue), *competition* (I win attitude with no compromise), *compromise* (give some, receive some to resolve the issue), and *collaboration* (working together).

Read the following scenario and decide where the five conflict styles were illustrated by noting the statements that identify each one.

Activity 6.3 Five conflict styles

Online team assignment – instructional plan for e-learners

Team A consists of Julie, Lynn, Paul, Bryant, and Anita.

Julie is the first to submit a response to the team, requesting to be the team leader for the week. She says that she will compile everyone's work. If everyone can select a section of the assignment to write, and submit it by Saturday, she will compile the paper. Lynn and Bryant respond, agreeing that Julie can be the team leader and deciding on the sections that they will write for the assignment. Paul joins the discussion a few days later and selects one of the remaining sections to write. Anita has to write the final section but does not check the team forum until three days later. She says that she does not want to write the final section and is upset because Julie took the lead.

Julie responds as follows: "Anita, I am sorry that you are not happy with your section but you should have logged in earlier because everyone has selected sections on the team. Dear, you have to take what is left."

Anita responses as follows: "Julie, you do not tell me when I should log in to the team. I had a family emergency. Would you have showed up to class online if your grandmother was in the hospital, not that it is any of your business. I am going to write the activities section for e-learners because that is where I have experience. Dear that!"

Julie does not respond at this point.

Bryant responds as follows: "Anita, that is my section, but you can have it. That is fine. I want this to go smoothly, so I will take the design model."

Anita submits the section she wanted and never acknowledges Bryant's kind gesture.

All the students submit their sections and Julie begins to compile the work.

Julie submits a message to the team forum: "Paul, you did not cite where you retrieved your sources. Please do so – I do not want us to get in trouble for plagiarizing."

Paul: "Julie, I am not good at citing sources. Can you cite them for me if I provide the web address and article information and tell you where they go? I can proofread the assignment before we submit it. I have a strong English background."

Julie: "That will work."

Julie submits the project for everyone to proofread. Paul proofreads first and then everyone acknowledges that the assignment is good to go. Julie, Lynn, Paul, Bryant, and Anita comment that the project looks fine.

Make every attempt to collaborate and work with your peers. Express clearly your ideas and do not automatically assume ill-intent. The antagonistic student might reject your attempts but at least you tried before reporting him or her to the instructor. The main point about communicating online or with any type communication is to consider the wording and the statements that you make; clear communication often determines the way the message is interpreted.

Activity 6.4 Communication with select groups

Take a moment to describe your communication with each of the following groups. What is the importance of professional communication in each area? What ethical issues could arise when interacting with each group?

- communication with course instructors
- communication with peers
- communication with school administrators.

Activity 6.5 Discussion questions

How do you think the method of communication would change during conflict with an instructor and peer online? Explain some ways to resolve conflict between course instructors, peers, and/or school administrators as an online student if any of the conflict styles were exhibited as shown in Figures 6.4–6.7.

Review the following instructor-to-student conflict scenario. Explain where the five conflict styles or communication strategies might help or hinder the situations in the online environment. Or, explain how you would resolve the conflict using what you learned in this course.

Instructor Basset

You submitted four of the same assignments for grading so slow down. I want you to do well. But, you have to submit work correctly to obtain good grades. Let me know if you have questions. I need one assignment to grade.

Student Henry

I am confused. You tell me to slow down, but you want me to resubmit my assignment. I had problems with my computer and did not know if I had submitted it. So, do you want me to submit them again or not?

Instructor Basset

Of course! I want you to submit your work. I was informing you what you were missing for week one assignment out of courtesy. You have submitted four files of the same type to the assignment section. I am not sure if you keep clicking the button but I was trying to help you before I grade on Wednesday. Follow the syllabus if you prefer that I do not comment to help you stay on track. That will help you with what is expected.

Student Henry

When I go into my assignments, I have submitted them correctly. I don't know why you are saying that they are the same assignment and I do not know what else you want.

Figure 6.4 Conflict scenario 1

Instructor McBride

Hi Team,

I received a message regarding confusion about the learning style assignment from your team member. I am not sure where the confusion lies but you should complete the assessment individually and rank your scores. The results are what you compile as a team on the assignment. I have provided an example below regarding how to complete the assessment.

Student Zhane

The confusion lies with what you are coming across as saying and how the instructions read. There are 20 questions on the assessment and three learning styles beneath them. I am not sure how to complete the assignment.

Instructor McBride

The confusion is not with me because I am not on your team so monitor your tone. Please email me privately with your concerns. Thank you.

Student Zhane

Instructor, I apologize if I offended you. You might have read more into my statements and received my tone incorrectly.

Instructor McBride

Show some respect in the main class area. I did not misinterpret anything regarding your statements. That is the last comment that I will provide to you about this because I do not keep interacting when students are disrespectful.

Student Zhane

I was not being disrespectful. I did not shout or use all caps. I find that I am having a difficult time communicating with

(continued)

you. I don't understand the assignment. I think that you are providing two different instructions. The book is explaining one way and you are explaining it differently, so I am confused on which way it should be done.

Team member C

Hello Instructor,

I really understand the assignment. Zhane wants me and the other team members to do it her way. I did it like your example. I don't know why she insists on completing it her way. Thanks for the example. I think she does not want to admit that she is wrong.

Team member C

Instructor, I am sorry to bother you with this again, but Zhane is sending me personal emails. She wants me to call her, and she is telling me that she was not trying to be rude, and she wants the assignment her way. I don't want anything to do with this. I'm not sure how to handle it. She is also making negative comments about you.

Zhane to team members

I'm not going to redo my assignment. I did it how our reading assignment said to do it and how the author of the assessment said it is to be done. If I am going to pay for these classes, I want to learn the right way. Please don't take what is being said as me being rude because that is not how I mean it. The instructor already misinterpreted what I was saying to her, which is why I prefer face to face or phone. I just don't like to put my name on something if I do not feel that it is correct. This virtual teamwork is difficult, and I want to be sure the instructor understands that her instruction is confusing.

Team member D

Zhane, you can look at this online experience as a great chance to learn how to express tone in your writing. It is really essential in business, in every form of writing, and of course essential in relating to the groups and instructors in college. I understand that you feel strongly about your opinion, but you might want to consider the instructor's example. In college, what the instructor will grade is what matters, correct?

Student Zhane

If you read our chapter reading assignment it reads different, check it out and let me know what you think. All I know about online tone is that capital letters or exclamation points show anger. I didn't do either of those.

Zhane calls the instructor and gets voice mail.

Instructor McBride

Per the voice mail message that you left on my phone, you seem to not be sure of the correct way to complete the learning style assessment and set on doing it your way. The only example and instruction is in the textbook and that is correct. I provided an example in your team. That is the way that it should be accomplished. It has been consistent for this class – for years that I have been teaching. Follow the example in the team forum and you will be fine. Ultimately, it is up to you.

Figure 6.5 Conflict scenario 2

Tom

Please do not take this the wrong way but your response should be about ethical dilemmas in an online classroom. You are discussing everything but that. Did you read the textbook material? I am not trying to be rude. The discussions can be difficult at times, and I am trying to help.

Eric

The instructor has not commented about my work. Perhaps you should mind your own business. Did you read the textbook material? Your example isn't all that great either.

Tom

I was simply trying to help.

Eric

Don't.

Figure 6.6 Conflict scenario 3

Ethics class

Sally

I personally believe that men are not as diplomatic as women about issues. For example, some men do not view diversity as a great contribution to projects and learning scenarios. Women tend to be more understanding and receptive of others' opinions.

Carlos

Did anyone else notice Sally's statement? I think that your statement is gender bias. How can you speak for all men?

Perhaps these are the men that you have encountered. I think diversity is great and the final product can be encompassing of many ideas. Can't you see how foolish your statement is?

Sally

Perhaps I was not clear. I was speaking in general. I really didn't mean that all men are not tolerant of diversity.

Carlos

Then why didn't you say that?

Figure 6.7   Conflict scenario 4

Personality types

Personality differences also have a lot to do with your behaviour with others, such as your peers and your instructors. When you bring a diverse group of individuals together, you are bringing different personalities together. Some personalities might not coexist well with one another. Online, this could be problematic in classes if there is a lack of understanding of personality characteristics to be displayed. One of the most popular *personality* indicators is the *Myers–Briggs Type Indicator® (MBTI®)* assessment tool. There are significant classifications of personality styles in this assessment. They are as follows: *introversion/extraversion – sensing/intuition – thinking/feeling – and judging/perceiving*:

- Introversion – people who exhibit this trait prefer working alone and generating thoughts from within.

- Extraversion – people who exhibit this trait prefer social interactions – sharing ideas and receiving ideas from others.

- Sensing – people who exhibit this trait prefer using their sensory perceptions such as hearing, feeling, and seeing to focus on the present situation.

- Intuition – people who exhibit this trait prefer focusing on patterns and impressions as well as their gut feelings.

- Thinking – people who exhibit this trait prefer to be objective and make decisions based on facts.

- Feeling – people who exhibit this trait prefer to be subjective and make decisions based on principles and values.

- Judging – people who exhibit this trait prefer to display characteristics of order and set schedules, and usually think sequentially.

- Perceiving – people who exhibit this trait prefer to display characteristics of flexibility and being adaptable. They rely on awareness and insight to decide on issues.

If you have a person who follows his or her intuition, who has urges and instincts to make decisions and complete assignments online, working with a person displaying the thinking type personality trait, who is basically analytical and making decisions on factual data, then conflicts and different perspectives will be present. You can actually select any personality style and compare and contrast similarities. People are different. The most important aspect about understanding personality traits is the *why* behind the behaviour. You cannot change a person, but you can learn to compromise and work cohesively, based on your knowledge that people do learn and behave differently.

Activity 6.6 Discussion questions

How can understanding personality traits help you as an online student? What are some strengths and weaknesses that could factor into interacting with diverse individuals and their personality styles?

How sensitive are you online?

It tends to matter, when you are involved in conflict, how sensitive you are regarding the issue and how you will respond. Rank your sensitivity level. Review your scores and determine if this is an area where you might need to improve by realizing that not every comment someone makes is a personal attack and that the person could really mean well:

1. If a peer commented about your work in class by suggesting that you do a spell check, would you be upset?

    Strongly disagree – disagree – somewhat – agree – strongly agree

2. If the instructor commented in class that you should read the textbook material to help you answer the question more efficiently, would you respond with a curt reply?

    Strongly disagree – disagree – somewhat – agree – strongly agree

3. If a peer comments that he or she has been reading your responses each week and has noticed a lack of effort and how you digress from the topic, would you send a flaming email?

    Strongly disagree – disagree – somewhat – agree – strongly agree

4. If a peer types, "I disagree with your statements and they have no scientific support," would you be upset?

    Strongly disagree – disagree – somewhat – agree – strongly agree

5. If an instructor emails you privately with your weekly feedback, commenting that the lack of effort and proofreading that you are showing in your work is disconcerting, would you respond by disagreeing?
   Strongly disagree – disagree – somewhat – agree – strongly agree

If your answers are mostly *agree* to *strongly agree*, you might want to work on not being as sensitive in class about students' or instructors' comments to you. Accepting feedback can produce growth as opposed to reacting to every statement that seems offensive – it might not actually be an offensive statement.

Activity 6.7 Good or poor student behaviour

Assess good or poor behaviour in an online classroom from peer to peer. Explain what you would do differently to resolve conflict based on what you learned, or if the response is fine and why. Would you elicit avoidance, accommodation, competition, compromise or collaboration?

Student A

If I cannot understand what I am expressing after proofreading my work, my audience will definitely not understand it – so this helps me. What do you do to ensure the reader can follow your points because it is obvious that you are not proofreading your work?

Student B

Please explain your work in your own words as opposed to using the Internet. You need to have some ideas presented in your answer – wouldn't you think?

Student C

I want to work with juvenile delinquents as well. Maybe you should narrow your subject to something more relevant to working with troubled youth.

Student D

Your contribution to the team is minimal. Also, you have not logged in to class in a while and we really need your input to complete the team assignment.

Student E

I thought long and hard before I sent this email, but you did not answer the discussion question correctly, even after the instructor posted an example of the way it should be done. Where is your mind?

Activity 6.8 Personality type displayed

Name the personality type that is predominantly being displayed by each person:

- David knows how to move the discussions forward. He engages the class with stories and ask his peers questions.
- Tina is very inquisitive. She asks her instructor questions to form clear ideas in the discussion forum in class. She also wants to ensure that she answers correctly, based on what she knows as facts.
- Yali has mapped a schedule for her assignments. She has prepared for each of the ten weeks of class by outlining the objectives and documented assignments for each week.

- Jann always concludes her responses with sincere remarks to her peers. She is always willing to assist them if they have any difficulties. She is quite sensitive to others' needs.

- San is reflective and shares a lot of personal stories in class. She enjoys online learning and the time alone on her computer.

- Sam has great instincts. He is able to compose tactful responses with good examples in class.

- Ann's responses usually show both sides of a situation. She prefers balance.

- Jules likes to discuss present-day issues and experiences. She enjoys hands-on work and is in tune with her surroundings and feelings.

Summary

Communication in your online classes is through correspondence. Therefore, it is important to compose diplomatic messages and remember that you are working with diverse groups and also that you are working with adults. Your messages can carry a tone, so selecting the correct words can make the difference in online communication. Communications with instructors and peers are the majority of messages in the online classroom. Individuals have different personality styles that can impact communication as well. When you are mindful of different styles of behaviour, you can be more tolerant of others in online classes. Applying conflict management strategies can help defuse disagreements.

What would you do?

How far will you go to prove your point in an online class in conflict with the instructor or peers? Do you understand when enough is enough and it is fine if you are misunderstood? Or will you do everything you can to explain your premise?

Figure 6.8 Self-reflection

Note

1. Thomas, K.W. and Kilmann, R.H. (1974, 2002, 2007) by CPP, Inc. *Thomas-Kilmann Conflict Mode Instrument.* All rights reserved.

7

Ethics boards: discussion responses

Abstract: Discussion forums are common both nationally and abroad for higher education at a distance. They are the main area where students answer discussion questions and interact with their peers. This is the main classroom and also an area where plagiarism occurs, intentionally and unintentionally. Intentional acts of plagiarism are viewed as deceptive actions, while unintentional ones are viewed as having no malicious intent from the student. If the student does not understand how to respond in the discussions, intentional and unintentional plagiarism occurs. It is not sufficient to tell students to complete class assignments and avoid plagiarism without a detailed review of how to do this successfully. The diversity of students and learning can influence acts of plagiarism. Some students simply might not understand how to compose a discussion response, how to avoid plagiarism, and the depth of reading involved in an online classroom. These topics are explored as well as student activities that have been included to consolidate the importance of avoiding plagiarism. This chapter concludes with Bloom's cognitive taxonomy and how it relates to composing answers to discussion questions.

Key words: discussions, Bloom's cognitive taxonomy, plagiarism.

Discussion interaction

Interacting in the *discussion* forums can be a daunting task for some students. Usually, online classes require students to answer weekly discussion questions as established in previous units. This is a general setup for some online courses. The discussion forum area is the section in class where students answer discussion questions by explaining what they have read, sharing experiences, and essentially showing what they have retained from the textbook material. This area is basically the main classroom. As an adult student, this is your time to shine. You can read what is required and then allow your peers and instructors to know you better. For example, if the topic is about time management, you can apply some strategies that you learned from the textbook and explain how time management has become a concern for you, given your many responsibilities as an adult learner. The discussion forum is not limited as long as you remain on topic, are diplomatic in your responses, and submit your own work by presenting your own ideas.

There have been instances where students have plagiarized in the discussion forums. What if this happened to you? What if a student's response is similar to yours? Would you blatantly comment to the student that, "You typed the same response that I typed and basically changed some words. You are a thief!" Is it an indicator that plagiarism has taken place because words are similar? Review the following scenarios that have occurred online in the discussion forums regarding plagiarism.

Case one

Roxy's book has not arrived in the mail; nor does she have access to the electronic textbook because she does not get paid until the end of the month. This is the second week of class. In the first week, the school provided courtesy chapters for students, but students are required to purchase their books. Roxy decides to formulate her answers based on other students' responses to meet her requirements for answering the weekly discussion question.

Activity 7.1 Discussion questions

How can you determine that Roxy's work is plagiarized if the words are not verbatim? What is wrong with Roxy's actions?

To avoid this happening to you, read others' responses and look for variations to see if students are forming their own opinions or forming their responses based on your work. If you have any concerns over repeated, similar responses, it is fine to contact your instructor so that he or she is aware that plagiarism is taking place. Some responses will be similar, but if you believe that your work is being plagiarized, it is a good idea to inform your instructor. You do not have to investigate and assume that your peers are copying your work, but usually there is no ambiguity around plagiarism if you are the author or producer of information. You will know when someone is copying your responses.

Case two

The topic for the week is about developing learning styles. Oscar is a visual learner and explains this well in his response. Oscar had visited several websites and a student chat room about learning styles. He was then able to use the words from these venues to explain how he learns.

Activity 7.2 Discussion questions

What advice do you have for Oscar with regard to forming his own opinion and applying critical thinking skills to answer discussion questions? What role did plagiarism play in Oscar's answer?

Not only could you be the victim of plagiarized work, but you do not want to be the offender. Monitor your use of the Internet for ideas. If you can read about your topic online, that does not excuse you from forming an opinion and expressing your own ideas.

Case three

Todd has been using the words of other students to answer his discussion questions. One week, he copied the exact words of his peer. When his peer commented that his responses were exactly like his statements, Todd commented, "Your response was good, so I decided to copy it." This was when the instructor noticed Todd's plagiarized offense. The student was contacted by the instructor. After the instructor reviewed previous weeks of the student's work, it was concluded that Todd had been plagiarizing other students' work, by changing a few words in some instances, for weeks. His response to the instructor was that people share the same responses and words of expression and that the instructor cannot assume that he plagiarized and it is simply the instructor's opinion.

There is never a time when students should use another peer's work, even if the other person is knowledgeable about work being used. It has occurred. It is illogical. It is plagiarism. Todd seemed to be oblivious to what he was doing and, when contacted by the instructor, appeared defensive, as if the instructor was imagining his plagiarism.

Not owning up to an offense is a sure way of being unsuccessful in school, repeating the same patterns, and stifling the growth process – that is not making the most out of the college experience.

Activity 7.3 Discussion questions

What plagiarism acts did the student Todd commit? What actions should the instructor take with regard to this student? What are your thoughts about this scenario?

Peer-to-peer plagiarism

Some topics in class will evoke similar responses from peers. However, words copied verbatim or rearranged usually show signs of *plagiarism*. And, when a student is copying another student, who is to say that the student being copied is submitting quality work and meeting the requirements? Review the following dialogue about career development and determine if you can decide where plagiarism has occurred.

Activity 7.4 Plagiarism scenario

- Question: how can time management help with career planning?
  - Don – in the student's case for this week's topic, utilizing technical tools available to plan and organize could be one step to help with time management and planning.
  - Patsy – career planning requires time management. Students have to set goals and track their progress. This is what I did when I returned to school.

- Giles – using technical tools will help with time management.

- Question: how does having a career plan serve as a guide for a career path?

  - Don – a career plan will serve as a guide because the student has a list of goals to reach to obtain the actual career.

  - Patsy – the main benefit of a career plan is that it provides a summary of small steps to be reached in order to advance from one goal to the next.

  - Giles – a career plan helps the student focus on what to do to obtain the career.

- Question: how can understanding personality styles help with career planning?

  - Don – personality styles can motivate the student as he or she progresses.

  - Patsy – when students understand their personality traits and those of others, they can select jobs that fit their personality and work more cohesively with others.

  - Giles – the student has a clear mind and is motivated by personality styles.

- Question: how can the student speaking with an advisor help with career planning?

  - Don – the student can discuss different programs available with his or her advisor.

  - Patsy – advisors often have resources that they can refer students to for career information.

  - Giles – the student can find out about programs needed for his or her career path.

Activity 7.5 Discussion criteria and rubric

Read the following passage and devise four discussion questions that you could possibly ask if you were the instructor. How would you expect students to answer the questions? Set the criteria and devise a grading scale worth five points for how you will grade the responses. What are your expectations for students answering the questions? An example of how to answer the questions is below the passage as well as an example in Figure 7.1 of the grading scale that you will create.

Workforce teams and the roles

People often comment about the importance of diversity in teams. In the workforce, diversity for team tasks is viewed as a way to generate ideas to create an effective product. The more ideas the better is often the mode of thinking for diversity in teams, but is it possible that personalities will clash, no matter whether there is diversity in a team or not? How can team members work together? How can you encourage members to participate in a team? Someone has to take the lead, not to serve as a dominator but to be an innovator for the team. Could this present an issue for other team members?

These are questions that are often asked and answered when team members begin to work together because they have diverse personalities. Some individuals have different work ethics, ages, and experiences that form their patterns of behaviour and solidify their interactions. Some team members work in haste while others are slow. This can influence team dynamics. There are certain roles that emerge on a team. The *aggressive role* is usually displayed by the individual who wants to control the assignment. The *passive role* is usually displayed by the individual who never takes the lead on the team or volunteers to help, but will help if acknowledged. The *slacker role* is usually displayed by the individual who does the minimum or nothing to help the team. The *I'll do it* role is usually performed by the individual who fulfills several responsibilities on the team, especially what the slacker refuses to do, to benefit the team. When the roles emerge, teams are unstable. In order for team members to work cohesively, each member must put in effort to complete assigned tasks and alternate as the leader, and everyone should submit ideas.

Answer example

I would expect a student to answer this as follows.

Working in teams is not easy. In order for members on a team to complete the task at hand, each member should contribute. There will be certain roles that will emerge on a team. As adults, we must try to implement goals and objectives so that particular roles won't be dominant, such as the aggressive role, or not helpful, such as the slacker role. In my work experience, I have interacted with passive members on teams. I often believe that I was more of the *I'll do it* player on the team and that left me frustrated. I am progressively learning to work with others and compromise.

Response was clear and related to the passage	Response applied relevant real-world experiences	Response advanced the discussions and was spell checked
2 points	1 point	1.5 points
Maximum = 2 points	Maximum = 1 point	Total = 4.5/5 points

Figure 7.1   Discussion criteria and grading

Keep in mind that as you interact in the discussions and form your ideas, there is probably a grading scale for discussion responses, as in Figure 7.1, that your instructor will provide in the class syllabus (class guide and expectations handout). Figure 7.2 shows another detailed sample grading

Applies course concepts, illustrates understanding of the assignment, and supports with research
Excellent Good Fair Poor
Interacts with peers regarding topic and adds value to the class in responses
Excellent Good Fair Poor
Applies relevant professional or personal experiences
Excellent Good Fair Poor
Uses correct grammar, spelling, and syntax
Excellent Good Fair Poor

Figure 7.2   Discussion criteria and grading example two

scale of the criteria that you could be assessed by in class for discussion responses.

Discussion question basic format

The basic format for answering discussion questions consists of the following:

- *Read* the required chapter material. Read the question.
- Determine (*dissect*) what the question is asking. Is the question multifaceted? If so, answer each part.
- Provide (*answer*) personal, tactful examples from your work history or personal experiences. Support your shared stories with textbook material.

Review closely what is included in the *read*, *dissect*, and *answer* format.

Read

Reading should not be underestimated online. You have to read the textbook to understand class content, read to help answer discussion questions, and read to understand the assignments. You also have to read the class expectations and rules as explained in previous chapters. When you read discussion questions and comprehend what the questions require, this increases your chances of obtaining a good grade and, of course, illustrating good ethical behaviour in class. Discussion questions usually include the content that is needed for you to research and this is a good time to implement critical thinking or a *critical analysis*. A critical analysis consists of an evaluation of the question as you form your opinions – you are assessing what the question is asking. You have to analyze the question to ensure that you have included the required components or answers. This is a result of reading carefully.

Dissect

When you dissect the question, you are in essence implementing the critical analysis. You are deciding what should be explored as in researching the question and how you will go about forming a comprehensible answer to the questions that are being asked. How you acquire the knowledge to answer the question and the level of detail that you provide to answer the question can be explained in Bloom's cognitive taxonomy. In 1956, Benjamin Bloom, along with a group of psychologists, developed a hierarchical classification of how people acquire knowledge. This concept has been around for years and is still an applicable framework in academia. It has also been revised with an abridged version by Anderson et al. (2001) and by others more recently. Basically, as individuals move up the learning pyramid, the level of learning becomes more advanced (see Figure 7.3). To apply Bloom's cognitive taxonomy to discussion questions and dissecting the question to form answers, the level of critical analysis is found in Bloom's cognitive taxonomy. Review the illustration.

Higher-level thinking skills

Evaluation
Synthesis
Analysis
Application
Comprehension
Knowledge

Lower-level thinking skills

Figure 7.3   **Bloom's cognitive taxonomy**

Source: Anderson, L.W., Krathwohl, D.R., Airasian, P.W., Cruikshank, K.A., Mayer, R.E., Pintrich, P.R., Raths, J. and Wittrock, M.C. *A Taxonomy for Learning, Teaching and Assessing: A Revision of Bloom's Taxonomy of Educational Objectives*, Abridged Edition, 1st,©2001. Printed and electronically reproduced by permission of Pearson Education, Inc., Upper Saddle River, New Jersey

Answer

When you answer the question, you could examine and weigh your answer against Bloom's cognitive taxonomy levels to determine if you are submitting quality responses.

The more advanced you are in your program, the more understanding you will gain about critical analysis in your work and Bloom's cognitive taxonomy. For this course, reviewing the basics of the hierarchy will help you begin to answer discussion questions.

Bloom's cognitive taxonomy

Knowledge

When you first look at the discussion topic, you could pose questions to yourself such as the following. What is my knowledge about the topic? What can I add? What can I document or have memorized about the topic? What do I want to know and what can I recall about the topic? What have I discovered about the topic to add to my answer?

For example, here is a discussion topic.

Provide an example of an issue that is legal but unethical, or an issue that is ethical but illegal. Describe any ethical ramifications about the issues.

Jose immediately begins to assess what he knows about the topic.

I was fired back in 2007 for no reason. I think that was unethical.

Comprehension

At the comprehension level, you can decide what can be described, explained, identified or reported about the topic.

I was living in the USA at the time and under the at-will policy. That is, I can get fired without a reason. It is legal but wrong.

Application

At the application level, you can pose questions to yourself such as: How can I apply, demonstrate, interpret, or practice what I am learning or have learned? This can help you compose answers that are of substance and transferable to your learning outside the classroom, such as in the workforce.

Now I understand I have to look for policies to protect myself from discrimination and that there are some exceptions to this at-will rule. To my peers, it is best to ask if you are under this policy at your company and read the clauses and stipulations to protect yourselves.

Analysis

You are advancing in your approach to answering discussion questions at the analysis stage. You are implementing answers that illustrate how you can categorize this information in real-life events, what distinguishes this information from what you already know, what questions it presents, and how additional research is applicable to you and your growth as a professional.

I have become quite knowledgeable about ethical and unethical practices in the workforce because of my ordeal. I am informed on the employee protection laws and this information has been transferable in my career.

Synthesis

This is a higher level of the hierarchy. At this stage, you are evaluating how can you formulate what you know and have learned, what new principles can be devised, and what can be constructed or created from these new concepts.

I have gained a wealth of knowledge because of my experiences. The reasons for termination should not consist of discrimination and bogus reasons for being fired because those are unethical practices in the workforce.

Evaluation

Finally, in the higher-level evaluation stage, you are evaluating how you can compare and contrast the information that you are learning. Can you predict any future outcomes, and how can you support your findings in your responses?

Peers, there is a central location where you can determine labor laws and if your state is under the at-will policy. I have attached it to my response.

The student has formed a clear answer, based on Bloom's cognitive taxonomy, to the ethical/unethical discussion topic.

Activity 7.6 Read, dissect, answer

Use the *read*, *dissect*, and *answer* format to answer the following discussion questions based on what you have learned throughout this course.

Discussion questions

Discuss ways in which your personal ethics and peer conflict can contribute to growth as an online learner. Describe some conflict resolution that you might incorporate in your own behaviour when interacting online.

Practice using Bloom's cognitive taxonomy with the same question from the Jose scenario (stated previously), but formulate a different response. Provide an example of an issue that is legal but unethical, or an issue that is ethical but illegal. Describe any ethical ramifications about the issues.

How can you use Bloom's cognitive taxonomy to help you answer the following discussion questions?

What are the characteristics of an ethical student in online classes? How can good or poor ethical behaviour contribute to collaborative learning? How might you help yourself meet your college goals by understanding your ethics and patterns of behaviour? This question is asking several questions. It is important to read, dissect, then answer while applying Bloom's cognitive taxonomy.

Summary

There is protocol to follow when answering discussion questions. If you follow a format, you are less likely to plagiarize material. Reviewing the grading scale for the discussions, so that you can understand the criteria and expectations for answering discussion questions, can help you meet expectations. Remember to read, dissect, and answer discussion questions to ensure that you are submitting quality responses. Bloom's cognitive taxonomy and measuring your responses against the hierarchy can help you assess your answers to questions and responses to peers. If you consider the quality of your work and place effort into submitting high-quality work, your answers to the questions in class and responses will merit being called scholarly level work.

What would you do?

How do you handle topics in class that are not interesting? Are you quick to search online for an answer instead of reading the textbook and trying to devise an answer?

Figure 7.4   Self-reflection

8

Adhering to principles: researching

Abstract: Since the inception of the Internet, research has been accessible. With accessibility comes the student's inclination to use sources that might not be as valid for research as other sources with extensive research. Research requires time and the searching of empirical data to form and support an opinion. Research requires students to become part of the scholarly field and contribute their ideas. Some students are often confused in this area. They do not understand how to approach research, paraphrase, and form opinions, often objectively. In the e-classroom, academic research is required for some assignments and students have to understand its validity. Credible research is not simply a click away online. Researching at the scholarly level requires commitment to assessing the data. Students will be introduced to scholarly research, the importance of asking epistemological questions, and stressors that can often influence quality research, and will participate in activities that allow them to explore these topics. The stress P example will provide some perspective on managing stress as an adult learner to submit quality work. This chapter concludes with a detailed review of quality writing in academia.

Key words: researching, writing, stress P example.

Research

As explained in Chapter 4, the comments from students who plagiarize essays reveal a lack of understanding of the writing process, not having enough time to complete class work, a lack of understanding that sources should be cited in an essay and on a reference page, and basically not understanding how to implement effective research. Researching to support the writer's premise in an essay is necessary for college writing and assignment submission.

How to research

Research – true research requires work. Research consists of supporting a position about a statement, with documentation of that support. It consists of generating new ideas to add to theory-based statements. Research essentially means *to search for, to find, to know.* Remember the days of microform machines in the library? This was the machine that housed articles. Using the card catalog to locate the article in microform was a difficult task. This might be dated for some of you! However, the student researcher would first have to visit the card catalog to find the related area on the topic in the microform system. Once the student located the topic, he or she went to the microform to review the article in small images called microfilm and to research and print articles. Sometimes, the articles were not what the researcher needed so he or she would have to start the same process to locate resources and other articles. This was laborious research but allowed for more accountability on the researcher's part. Since the inception of the Internet, the accessibility and convenience factors are favourable for researchers.

However, there are websites that are not credible and should not be used in a scholarly setting such as college. Using a source because it is the first website retrieved from search results is a sign of being lax. Research takes time. It takes time to read what is on the web page, research the author, and research other related material, such as primary sources (the original work usually referenced at the bottom or side of a web page), to locate substantial, quality, credible support for your premise in your work. This is not accomplished in ten minutes, simply because the Internet is a great place to search. College is synonymous with writing essays. The student must be responsible for the integrity of his or her work, and in research avoid plagiarism and apply critical thinking. John Lake (2011), instructor for the University of London International studies and novel writer, commented the following about plagiarism and writing:

> The issue of plagiarism, it seems to me, comes to revolve around a student's ability as a writer, and not necessarily around the student's proclivity for critical thinking. The argument might go that students can copy a description of Einstein's Theory of Relativity into an essay, but that doesn't prove that they understand it. The ability to paraphrase, to express the theory *in their own words*, thus becomes a yardstick of comprehension.

Comprehending the material when researching and forming ideas about the research are the approaches to initiate the writing process and avoid acts of plagiarism. You will review some writing strategies in this chapter. Some college students use articles from online encyclopedias and community websites for research. This is because these websites are easily searchable. However, encyclopedias were fine to use for grade and high school papers. At the college level, research is more involved. There is a misconception that since the Internet, research is easy. In fact, Internet research can be more laborious than visiting the library for a book, given the amount of search results and locating credible articles, which no doubt requires work and effort.

Writing effective quality papers requires credible research in order to obtain good grades. This has not changed simply because web resources can be used and text easily copied. It is wise to use web resources that are retrieved from educational and government websites. There are online journals that specialize in topics and non-profit organizations that can benefit student research as well. When you are using your school's library, review the educational journals and then visit their websites. You can find quality information to support your ideas. Some libraries online have academic databases from the following organizations with valid articles. There are several to choose from, depending on your topic, but here are some popular academic databases with quality articles: Routledge: Taylor and Francis Group, Sage Journals Online, EBSCOhost, and ProQuest. Library services are usually part of the school's resources available to you for research.

You can also research the author, if he or she is listed on the source, Google the author and note any other publications that he or she might have created or any governing affiliations. Reputable media websites are great for research. It is wise to avoid websites that are simply opinion based and are dated. Also, blogs, wikis, dictionaries, and other community websites are not scholarly and should be avoided for college work.

Be scholarly in your research

In order to be scholarly in your research, you have to look for scholarly information and devise scholarly statements about your perspectives. You might have heard of a hypothesis in science classes. A hypothesis is an educated guess (you might have heard that definition) or a hypothesis is a tentative explanation that should be tested by collecting data and research. For example, if you had to write about distance education classes, your hypothesis could be as follows: students need advanced computer and reading skills to prepare for online classes.

Then, you could test your hypothesis by researching any articles or studies in this area that could help support your premise. You may or may not be correct. That is the purpose of researching the hypothesis.

There are two types of data to be aware of when researching: *qualitative* data and *quantitative* data. Qualitative data is described with statements and qualitative research consists of information from observations and interviews. For example, if a researcher compares learning styles in different cultures, he or she might conduct interviews with students and then summarize findings from the interviews. Quantitative data is described with numbers; for example, IQ tests that produce quantitative data, and surveys where the researcher questions a specific sample of a population and summarizes the results in percentages or numbers of some sort. Basic research requires you to review quantitative and qualitative studies and support your findings with your new ideas, concepts, or even theories about a topic. Thus, you are starting to build scholarly skills for researching and writing.

Stephen Brookfield, author and professor, defined critical research as asking epistemological questions. "When students ask epistemological questions of text, they want to find out how an author comes to know that something is true. Epistemological questions inquire about what writers regard as acceptable grounds for an assertion of truth" (Brookfield, 1995).[1]

Review some sample questions that are epistemological in nature.

For example, if you read that research shows that online students are over the age of 35, epistemological questions would consist of asking where this information was retrieved. Where is the background information regarding any studies that could confirm the age of adult learners? Why did the author make this statement and what type of support is evident in this information? Epistemological questions should be composed when researching and trying to ensure that the information you present in your essays and work is valid. As college students, you are learning to apply critical thinking to research and your work. Epistemological questions evoke critical thinking. You are no longer accepting the words on the page but becoming more of an investigator and researcher of your own work and ideas. You are adding to the literature that is presented by forming and supporting your own perspectives.

Passive or ownership positions – technology

With the fast-paced society that has plagued our generation, has technology influenced the lax attitude and effort with regard to substantial research? What position has technology created for the user regarding his or her responsibility for assignments and research? Has a passive position resulted as a direct result of technology? Has an ownership shift of work increased as a direct result of technology? Review the following scenarios with regard to research, plagiarism, and essay development. Ponder these questions and comment on them in your discussions this week.

Case one: Sammie's senses

Sammie has been completing work for her husband in the military for three weeks. She emails the instructor to explain that Brent, her husband who is enrolled in the course, was in the field in Iraq. He could not complete the work or be reached. For three weeks she has been completing his assignments and wanted to know what she could do for an alternative assignment for him since he missed a live session with the instructor. The instructor informed Sammie that this is plagiarism. She should not have been submitting his work for three weeks or ever. She is also not enrolled in this course so it is inappropriate to discuss his work. Sammie sends an email and says no, it isn't plagiarism because he is on the telephone telling her what to type. This is the only week he isn't available to tell her what to type and that the instructor doesn't understand. They are married. Sammie has an undertone in her email of "what is the big deal?"

Activity 8.1 Discussion questions

What is wrong with Sammie's actions? What role did technology play in Sammie being able to complete her husband's work for three weeks? What is your position about technology or Sammie in this response? Is the onus on Sammie, her husband, or technology?

Case two: Allegra's allegory

Allegra Volesta submitted her persuasive essay in the name of Tim Levin. The instructor emails Allegra, asking her to resubmit her paper and explaining that she submitted the paper in another person's name. The instructor was giving Allegra the opportunity to reflect on her dishonesty and redeem herself. Allegra acknowledges the mistake and resubmits the same paper in her name. She simply removed Tim Levin's name off the paper.

Activity 8.2 Discussion questions

Is it possible in dishonesty to lose common sense? What were the ethical implications in this scenario? Do you think that the student assumed that the instructor would not catch the error? Do you believe that unethical decisions are part of the human condition? What are your thoughts? What role did being an online student and this being an online class have in Allegra's actions?

Activity 8.3 Internet search

Review the Internet for a website that can be used in academic work and a website that cannot be used in academic work. Explain why you decided on your choice. Address any epistemological questions that you could ask or might factor into using the website.

Activity 8.4 Passive or ownership scenario

Passive or ownership positions

Create a scenario when a student might take a passive and ownership position in his or her school work due to technology. Provide one example for each. Present any ethical dilemmas that could result from either position.

Activity 8.5 Quantitative and qualitative data

Select a topic to research. Choose two articles about the topic, one quantitative, and the qualitative data in your school's library. Summarize your findings and explain why it is important to support your work with both types of data in college.

How to write

It is not sufficient for instructors to inform a student to avoid plagiarism and not explain how to do this when writing in the discussions or writing essays. For discussions, it is important to read the required textbook material explained in your course each week. That is the only way to ensure that you have an informed opinion and answer, unless you have knowledge about the topic. You reviewed how to answer the discussions and composed a discussion grading rubric in Chapter 7. You also reviewed how to apply critical analysis to your answers. This area focuses on the writing process when composing discussion responses and essays.

For example, if you are required to read the following passage about stress and time management, a quality written response would be as explained below the passage.

Stressed out in college

Students often comment about being stressed out in college. They have many responsibilities and find it difficult to complete class work. Sometimes poor time management can result in stress for the student. Lack of finances and job transitions are also stressors for the adult learner. Events will occur in life to provoke stress. How do adult learners prevent the stress and anxiety overwhelming them to the point of not completing class work and their degree goals? Following the illustration below might provide some guidance. The *stress P example* in Figure 8.1 is a great way to compartmentalize stressors. Ideally, students should be at

---

Stressors

Jobs > Finances > Classes > Relationships > Children > Unexpected issues

Point of worry

How long will you allow yourself to worry about the issue? What is in your power to control must be assessed. If you cannot control the outcome, you should try to reduce the stress to a practical approach.

Point of focus

How can you focus on the point? Some issues are not as difficult to stay focused on. When there are health matters or family issues, it is best to allocate time for the stress and anxiety and then at least contribute one hour to work daily. That is one of the most effective ways to see progress in the midst of stressors. Practicing staying focused consists of allowing yourself time to worry about the issue and then redirecting your thoughts to what needs to be accomplished.

Point of positivity

This is the ideal level to minimize stress. The question posed at this level is "What must be accomplished?" Realistically review what must be accomplished. Realize that what must be accomplished should be done and could eventually be part of the resolution for the current stressor.

Figure 8.1   Stress P example

the bottom of the example where stress levels are low and not at the top where stress levels are extremely high.

The bottom of the stress P example is where stress is controllable. Students should try to manage the stress or stressors in order to obtain positive results. Stressors are inevitable. Following the stress P example and trying to manage stress can really help adults reach college goals. If students truly believe that they have a destiny, hopefully the stress will not deter them. Stress is only a night season.

Good discussion responses

Example A

I thought the information on stress management and college students was informative. I can relate because I am a college student. Some days I have certain stressors such as taking care of my child and having to work, so that I am not motivated to complete class assignments. The stress P example was helpful. I like the statements that I should compartmentalize stress and that I should prioritize my tasks. I also like allowing myself time to work and time to worry if needed. I believe I can accomplish more if I do not let stress overwhelm my goals.

Example B

I did find some of the information from the textbook helpful regarding stress management. However, I usually manage my stressors well. I prioritize tasks, and I have never been the type of person to worry. The stress P example referenced staying focused. I usually commit to my goals when I decide that I must complete them. One practice that I have applied that was not mentioned in the reading material was meditation. Meditation has worked for me. I take ten minutes out of the day to clear my mind. It seems to help me stay focused and recommit myself to my goals. Do any of my class members have any strategies to share regarding stress management?

The first two responses are totally different. However, they both share information from the passage and their own perspectives. Example B student asked classmates a question in an attempt to advance the topic. That is how discussions and starting the writing process should work. It is your time to highlight how the textbook material and research applies to you.

Poor discussion responses

Example A

I enjoyed reading about the stress P example. I am always stressed out and I am looking for ways to better manage my time.

Example B

I think stress is part of adults' lives. I did not understand the relevance of this passage.

Notice that neither response expanded on information from the passage or personal information. Student B did not agree with the passage and that is fine. But, the student did not elaborate on why he or she did not agree and thus the response is curt and does not advance the discussion.

Grammar tips

Equally important in writing are grammar and syntax. It is admirable to relearn grammar rules if you struggle in this area as an adult learner. You can visit your school's writing lab for grammar handouts or search online. Grammar Girl (*http://grammar.quickanddirtytips.com/*) and Purdue (*http://owl.english.purdue.edu/*) are great websites to learn basic grammar rules. You can obtain free material at your school because online schools usually have a writing center with resources. Grammar takes years to learn; it is important that adults attempt to learn the rules in the event they were missed in grade and high school. This is not an easy task, but progressive steps make a difference in college writing.

Figure 8.2 shows some common mistakes in college writing. It is important to be mindful of these points.

Avoid contractions in essays – spell the word
Instead of couldn't, write could not
Instead of don't, write do not
Instead of haven't, write have not

Commonly confused words

A lot is two words	Than refers to comparison
There refers to location	Then refers to at that time or following
Their refers to people	Threw – past tense of throw
All ready means prepared	Through – from one side to the other; complete
Already means previously or before	To = toward Too = also or excessive Two = number

The correct statement is as follows:

It is *because* he arrived late that the meeting was interrupted.

The incorrect statement is as follows:

It is *cause* he arrived late that the meeting was interrupted.

(continued)

Verb person and number

	Singular	Plural
1st person	I jog	we jog
2nd person	you jog	you jog
3rd person	he, she, it jogs	they jog

Essays should be written from the third-person point of view, unless they are narrative essays about your personal experiences. A narrative should be written from the first-person point of view. When in doubt, ask your instructor. Avoid second-person point-of-view references in essays.

Commas

Some usages of commas include setting off introductory clauses, separating items in a series, using on both sides of a dependent clause, and using between two complete sentences connected by coordinating conjunctions such as for, and, nor, but, or, yet, and so.

College writing versus casual writing

College writing consists of formal language and structure. There is form in college writing and proper sentence structure. Casual writing consists of informal language. Slang and jargon-related terms are accepted in casual writing. Casual writing usually occurs between friends and acquaintances. Casual writing is not college writing and should be avoided in college. This includes not using text language.

Place endings on words. For example, the correct word is doing not doin and going not goin.

The letter (I) should be capitalized when used as a single word. Punctuation should be used consistently.

Avoid double negatives.
I am *not* learning *nothing* in this course. Incorrect
I am *not* learning *anything* in this course. Correct
I am *not* doing *nothing* today. Incorrect
I am *not* doing *anything* today. Correct

Figure 8.2 Grammar examples

Other important tips

- Read and take notes.

- Annotate ideas.

- Paraphrase information and cite the source.

- Write your ideas immediately.

- Be conscientious and record reactions to your research and what you read to form ideas.

- Analyze the material that you read to apply critical thinking and critical reading. Some questions that you could ask yourself to generate ideas and compose responses are as follows:

  - Do I agree with what the information is presenting?

  - Are there enough facts to support the main idea of what is being presented?

  - How would I have expressed my ideas on the topic?

  - What can I add to this material?

  - Is the material presented in a logical style?

Written assignments – essays

When you have to write an essay, it is important to research the material and form your own opinion about what you researched. You should use your own words and not the paraphrased words of someone else for the majority of the essay. That can be difficult when you are not a subject matter expert but a student writer. Yes, you will need citations or others' factual data to support your premise, but the introduction, the setup in the body to another person's work, and conclusion in an essay should be your work. Review the basic essay writing example in Figure 8.3 for help.

Introduction for a paper Thesis statement = the main idea of the passage composed in a clear sentence about what is to be discussed Then, three points to be discussed about the topic
Body Your words in detail about the three points in the introduction to be discussed here, a citation, your words, a citation, your words, a citation then more of your words. Your words should consist of your opinion about the material that you read or researched from an objective perspective – third-person point of view
Conclusion Summary of your thoughts. This should be accomplished in the third-person point of view as well. You can add *new* insights to what was learned about the three points as you conclude the paper.

Figure 8.3   Basic essay writing example

It is prudent to remember that if an instructor wanted to read Internet words, he or she would surf the web independently. Using Internet facts and statements in a student assignment, with no ideas represented from the student, is simply the incorrect way to write and could quickly result in a plagiarized work, an unethical decision. You have to cite (document) where you received the information. Based on your research, you can start to write your ideas and arguments and then support with citations. Use examples and cite subject matter expert's research sparingly to create a strong essay.

Activity 8.6 Writing and plagiarism scenario

Review the following responses to the question. Determine where plagiarism has occurred and explain how you could determine that it has taken place.

What kinds of technical skills do you need to perform proficiently when working as an advanced help-desk specialist?

Reza

I perform troubleshooting on connectivity issues. I perform resetting passwords but mostly troubleshooting during the day. They only call me when the end users are having problems.

Alice

The following skills are needed:

- Be responsible for diagnostic data domain de-duplication systems on a daily basis.
- Isolate, reproduce and track bugs and verify fixes.
- Conduct Webex to reset logs DNS replications re-sync.
- Reset user credentials.
- Check performance recommend upgrades.
- Contribute to knowledge base articles.
- Assist field engineers to log in to systems to verify part verification status after replacement.
- Decode logs and bios.txt for hardware failures.

Sherman

Some skills to perform the technical job include collecting the required documents and organizing, evaluating, and calculating data for the company. I have worked in this position for the past five years and the routine is consistent each day.

Thesis statements

A thesis statement is a sentence that describes the main idea of your subject. It describes what you want to say and prove in your essay or writing. When you have a clear thesis statement, it helps with what you want to research about the topic. A good thesis statement is debatable and specific, and provides guidance in your essay.

Poor thesis statement

I want a career in education when I graduate.

Good thesis statement

Educational leadership positions are successful jobs in higher education.

(From this thesis statement, you can determine that the paper will focus on educational leadership positions in college and what educational leaders do in academia.)

Poor thesis statement

I enjoy being a college student.

Good thesis statement

College is challenging, yet having a degree will present more job opportunities.

(From this thesis statement, the student will discuss some of the challenges of being in college and share possible job opportunities that can occur as a result of having a degree and job titles.)

Poor thesis statement

Women are dominating.

Good thesis statement

Women have taken roles in the family and workforce that have produced challenges in relationships. (This paper will discuss issues that women encounter in the workforce that could influence their behaviour in relationships.)

Practice how to write and form opinions.

Step one

Your topic is about writing and technology. If this topic is unfamiliar to you, start by asking yourself some questions. This can help you generate ideas to initiate the writing process. Some questions to consider are as follows:

- How has technology impacted writing?
- What are some of the advantages and disadvantages of using the computer to write a paper?
- What are the length requirements of the paper?
- How do I feel about technology/writing?
- What can I say about emails, text messaging, and blogging in my paper?

You can always take parts of a topic that are familiar to you and expand on those to develop paragraphs. This will produce a guide for your writing and help you explore other areas when you start to research. Once you gather some ideas, you are ready to begin research to aid in composing your draft.

Step two

Now, say for instance that you do find an article on your school's online library that will work for support in your paper. You are ready to begin writing about this topic. Review the article below. Following the article, you will look at two students' responses as they begin to write their essays. Then, you will formulate your own response.

Discussion nightmares! What role does technology play? by McBride and Smith (April 2009)

The role of formal writing is declining at a rapid rate in distance education courses. The invention of technical gadgets has inadvertently had an effect on the way students compose their responses in the discussion question forums, in class. Lowercase letters, incomplete sentences, and text language are becoming the normal way some students write. This article addresses these issues as well as offering suggestions for educators to solve this problem.

It seems that instant and text messaging have made their way into higher education – distance learning. The i, 2, u, plz, and thx are becoming standard parts of students' discussion responses in online classes. Imagine being out of school for close to ten years, as some adult learners have been, and having to learn a structured way of writing. Imagine graduating from high school and being accustomed to using technical gadgets, and not knowing that a certain vernacular is not accepted in college. It is challenging for students who have been out of school for long periods of time to write in the discussion forums. It is equally challenging for young adults graduating from high school, who have easily acclimated to technology, to write effectively in the discussion forums. It seems that each group needs retraining on basic writing skills in college.

Now, setting standards for writing is more difficult because of the use of abbreviated words and an over-usage of lowercase letters that might be the result of instant and text messaging. A lowercase (i) will seep into more than half of the class responses when (I) is the correct spelling used as a single word. Also, not capitalizing the first word of each sentence is problematic, as well as run-on sentences and disdain for punctuation. Essentially, all text is being typed in lowercase. Jargon such as "haha" and "lol" have become the normal typed text. They have replaced phrases such as, "I smiled when I read your response" or "that made me laugh."

The inclination to want to spell a word correctly or use a dictionary is almost archaic. Misspelled and quick words have replaced efficient messages. What does this mean for a competitive workforce, an error-free résumé, and verbal and written communication during an interview for potential graduates? What does this mean for potential online students if the alumnus is instantaneously criticized because he/she cannot compose an email to his/her supervisor or the CEO of a company, translating an important message? It means that someone is out of work. It means that someone cannot express him/herself verbally during an interview efficiently without jargon-related phrases. It means that someone is not cognizant that he/she has poor written and verbal communication because it is now visceral.

What is happening to grammar, syntax, and proofreading? Are these qualities in writing diminishing at rapid rates? Are discussion question responses submitted in haste like a text message? Is technology really the catalyst behind this movement? Or, is it the individual who has become lax and careless with his/her message by taking the convenience of technology for granted? If the answers to these questions receive indifference from educators, then the value of writing is off-kilter.

Technology has made life convenient; that statement is pervasive. But the convenience does not excuse placing forth the required effort into knowing how to do the work without the desired technology. Sometimes computers do not work and a manual process is needed. If a person cannot write using the manual process when the computer is down, businesses and tasks become powerless. The point is simple – the significance of writing, and writing effective messages, cannot be obsolete. The path to this is *not* simple. Educators will need to take the lead. Students will need to take learning seriously and do the work. Online instructor Jean White (2009) explains that this writing style is prevalent among younger adults, "It seems to be occurring with the younger students who are used to text messaging. I notice it especially with students just beginning their academic program."

Will the next businessman be able to negotiate or proofread his business deal in writing? This poses more questions than answers. Some students (young and old) are well educated, have great writing skills, and can articulate themselves flawlessly; attending school online and writing in class appears effortless. But, writing is problematic for other students. The question remains posed, "Will the next businessman be able to negotiate or proofread his business deal in writing with poor grammar?" The answer is an emphatic no! A good deal has gone awry because of thx, u, 2 to name a few.

This is college! This is academia! The degradation of writing must be addressed. Online instructors must enforce the standards to preserve the legacy of higher education. Online instructors are not the only initial contact for online students. Advisors, instructional/curricula designers, and administrators must set the standards as well. Advisors could remind students of the importance of writing in online classes and about the writing services that schools have available, if this is problematic for individuals. Having potential online students write a couple of paragraphs in the prescreening stage might help target individuals who struggle in this area before being enrolled in an English composition course. For those who manage to construct the paragraphs without errors but have problems later in class, online instructors could take the lead by sending messages to students about the correct way to compose their messages without the shortcuts, as well as provide additional resources. Sometimes, the student simply needs to be made aware of when to use lowercase letters and when to spell a word correctly – or to simply proofread.

Instructional/curricula designers and administrators must factor grammar and syntax into grading policies. There should be a range of points for discussion responses where grammar mechanics could be included in the grading policy. Students should not receive full points for poorly constructed responses. Asking a student what he/she is trying to convey might be another viable approach to initiate a writing process, or at least a concern for presenting quality work.

Teaching adult students to be proactive in their learning is part of being an online instructor. There are numerous credible, free resources online for students to relearn basic grammar rules if they have forgotten them. There is help available in and out of school to promote effective writing.

Some students will do the minimum amount of work if these issues are not addressed. Grades must reflect the negligent responses and lack of effort that have replaced the value of obtaining a college degree.

Technology will continually change. The state of the economy, employment rates, and college enrollment will stagger yet improve. Will college students be prepared with effective communication skills to adapt to these changes? Will college students be able to compose a comprehensible paragraph? Will college students convey their messages? If not, distance education will fail fast; this cannot happen.

Student A's essay introduction

Rigid rules are needed for students writing in distance education. The lax effort in students' writing is becoming problematic online. Has technology played a role in the decline of formal writing or is it the student writer's responsibility to ensure his or her work is of quality? These are the topics that will be discussed.

McBride and Smith (2009) explained that technology is readily accessible but cannot be the main proofreader for a writer. "Technology has made life convenient… But the convenience does not excuse placing forth the required effort into knowing how to do the work without the desired technology… the significance of writing and writing effective messages cannot be obsolete in academia" (para. 6). The student writer has to put in the effort to proofread his or her work. Technology makes it easier to type responses and obtain a college degree. However, it is wise to use technology for the advantages and not for the disadvantages to communicate effectively. This statement essentially means avoiding text language in college writing.

Activity 8.7 Discussion questions

Notice student A's response. The student forms her own introduction and introduces the author's quotation before using it. Then, the student closes the paragraph with her ideas. What do you think about student A's beginning of the article? What is the thesis statement?

Student B's essay introduction

Technology could be the reason why writing is declining in college. Text language is now part of formal writing in higher education. This has inadvertently affected writing at the collegiate level. A lowercase (i) will seep into more than half of the class discussion board responses when (I) is used as a single word. Also, not capitalizing the first word of each sentence is problematic as well as run-on sentences and disdain for punctuation. Essentially, all text is being typed in lowercase. Jargon such as "haha" and "lol" have become the normal text. They have replaced phrases such as, "I smiled when I read your response" or "that made me laugh" (McBride and Smith, 2009, para. 3).

Notice Student B's response. The first sentence was the student's original work and the rest of the information is from the article. Is this a plagiarized response?

Activity 8.8 Essay paraphrase

Write two to three sentences about the topic, either in support of technology benefiting writing in college or against technology and formal writing. Then, use a quotation or material from the essay to support your sentences. Remember, your thoughts should make up the majority of the sentences, not McBride and Smith's material. Also, you must credit the authors as in the examples provided when you use their words.

Activity 8.9 Essay writing

Now, write your own summary of the article "Discussion nightmares! What role does technology play?" As indicated in the students' responses above, you can support with information from the article, but you must cite the source and not plagiarize. Try summarizing your own ideas and thoughts regarding this article and topic.

Activity 8.10 Plagiarism reasons

Review the following five general statements. Select the one that you think best describes the reason why you think students plagiarize. Support your answer based on what you have learned from this material:

- Students plagiarize because they are lax in doing the research and work.

- Students plagiarize because they do not understand how to write essays.

- Students plagiarize because they are working adults with limited time for class work.

- Students plagiarize because they think that they will not get caught.

- Students plagiarize for a variety of reasons.

Remember that your answers to the discussion questions and your essays permit occasions to explore your own thoughts and share your insights with others. Avoid plagiarism in your work. You have ideas and a voice that should be heard. Remember Allegra? What was she thinking?

Summary

Researching requires effort. Students should conduct research online using credible websites such as educational journals and the school's library resources. There are two types of data that can be used to support work in academia. They are quantitative and qualitative data. The lack of understanding of the writing process and research can result in plagiarism. Learning or relearning basic grammar rules is often required at the adult level to submit scholarly level work. Developing grammar skills and learning how to compose a clear thesis statement are steps in the right direction to enhance writing skills. The more knowledge a person has of how to compose essays and responses, the fewer chances there are that plagiarism will occur. Understanding how to evaluate data and ask specific epistemological questions allows you to be informed as the student researcher. Technology is resourceful, but students have to take an ownership role regarding their work.

What would you do?

Do you think that stress can lead to desperation to meet a goal and you making unethical choices? How would you handle a stressful = desperation class assignment scenario?

Figure 8.4   Self-reflection

Note

1.   Reprinted with permission of John Wiley & Sons, Inc.

9

Critical thinking

Abstract: Critical thinking for the adult learner can very well signify success or failure of the degree goal. Internal factors such as fear, emotions, and reflections of experiences can impact decision making. External factors such as social media, friends, and literature can also impact decision making. The circle of influences creates pressure on the logical or illogical thought process and can be counterproductive when initiating a critical thinking process. In this chapter, a list of comments from students provides diverse perspectives about the connection between critical thinking and ethics. Students will engage with the critical thinking circle and activities that examine critical thinking in the online classroom in detail. This chapter concludes with information about internal and external factors that influence critical thinking and ethical decisions that online students encounter.

Key words: critical thinking circle, ethics, time management.

Critical thinking and unethical decisions

If critical thinking calls for a decision-making process as established in Chapter 3, can the same decision-making process be applied when making unethical decisions? Often when reflecting on critical thinking and its concepts, it is natural to think that it is exercised when making informed decisions. What about when a student decides to plagiarize?

Is critical thinking implemented to make a poor choice? Consider the following scenario regarding critical thinking using the Internet.

Case one

Angela has family in town for the weekend, and she has a paper due on Monday. She is mindful of the paper because she tries to write an introduction but then is interrupted when the family wants to see the town's tourist attractions. She takes her family on a tour of the city and out to dinner. When she arrives home, she thinks about the paper but decides to complete it tomorrow, but tomorrow arrives and she is still entertaining the family. It's Sunday afternoon and Angela is not in the mindset to write a paper so she searches online for ideas about her topic and discovers a website that has a paper written about it. After reading the paper, Angela concludes that the paper is excellent. She wonders whether she will get caught if she changes a few words and uses the paper as her own. She thinks about receiving a zero and concludes that there is a 50/50 chance of her passing or failing. She rationalizes that the instructor might not realize that it is an Internet paper so she decides to use it.

Activity 9.1 Discussion question

Did Angela apply critical thinking to decide on using the Internet paper? She followed what could be considered a thought process. She was lucid, systematic in her thoughts, and considered the outcomes. She thought outside of her parameters by reasoning that the instructor would possibly not notice the plagiarized work to help her make her choice. She created scenarios about possible outcomes.

Some elements of critical thinking can be applied even when the result is a poor choice or the results are not what you hoped, despite the fact that a significant amount of research supports applying critical thinking when making good choices. Perhaps Angela did not factor in rational thinking and therefore did not meet all the requirements of critical thinking. In college, applying critical thinking can make the difference to submitting class work on time (time management) or composing an offensive message to your peers or instructors. Critical thinking in college can make a difference between passing and failing, and even to plagiarizing. Ideally, critical thinking is applied to ethical decisions when completing assignments and making good choices. The challenge reverts to what is considered ethical or not for each individual as examined in this book.

John Lake (2011), instructor for the University of London International studies and novel writer, commented the following about ethics:

> There is the question of cultural relativity to be addressed. It is a fact that overseas students are now crucial to the financial lifeblood of academic institutions in the UK and the USA, for instance, and their circumstances need to be taken into consideration. With regard to the topic of academic citation, what is regarded as ethical may differ considerably between nationalities, societies and entire global regions. Some cultures view it as ethically *wrong* to alter the wording of authoritative texts, most notably China, so strategies for avoiding morphological co-construction – what 'the West' sees as plagiarism avoidance – might well represent a cause for penalisation in certain non-Western education systems.

Ultimately, you have to decide as the student and inform yourself about *ethical* practices under the organization and the concept of critical thinking. As you gain more knowledge, your choices and perspectives about ethics might evolve.

Critical thinking and time management

Often, students comment about not having enough time to complete class work. They are working mothers and fathers, experiencing job transitions, dealing with finances, and handling several issues that play a significant role in *time management*. There are no magic rules for completing class work and balancing school, work, and family commitments. Planners can help. Using technology to your advantage can also help, such as cellular phones as task reminders and computer calendars. Ultimately, you have to decide on a schedule that works for you, that allows you to complete assignments and manage your other adult responsibilities. Identifying productive times to work is wise. Allocating time for class work only is a good strategy. Answering discussion questions or interacting with peers in the discussion during lunch time can help. Reading course material while waiting on appointments is also a great way to maximize small amounts of time. You have to do what works for you by applying critical thinking to your time management.

Activity 9.2 Time management plan

How would you manage a schedule based on the following scenario? What would you do? How can Harry apply critical thinking to time management?

Harry is returning to school online. He has a 16-year-old son. He is working at a job with no career advancement and his hours are 9 a.m. to 7 p.m. He returned to school so that he can provide a better life for his child as well as enjoy a fulfilling career.

He has to get his son from football practice when he leaves work. He is really not motivated to complete class work. In theory, it all sounds great – the working on the degree to advance himself. But, he is exhausted. The job that he does not like consumes a lot of his time. On the weekends, he wants to relax and spend time with his son as opposed to completing class work.

Critical thinking and discussions

As explained in this book, applying critical thinking to answer discussion questions actually requires reading the textbook material, researching, and then composing clear thoughts to answer the question. Often, students try to finesse the answers by not reading the material and typing some random response to submit work and it shows. Critical thinking in the discussions requires you to question the material and form your own opinion. You have opinions that should be diplomatically stated in your responses. Critical thinking in the discussions requires you to problem-solve or devise a plan of approach and resolution to the topic or class content. Critical thinking in the discussions requires you to apply Bloom's cognitive taxonomy to assess your answers to discussion questions. It takes effort to apply critical thinking to your discussion responses.

Activity 9.3 Habitual liar

Suppose you had a friend who was a habitual liar. Every encounter with your friend was like a scene from the movie *Big Fish*. Basically, your friend tells an elaborate story with no reason or logic whenever he is in dialogue with you. Instead of listening to his stories and accepting them as truth, perpetuating the problem, you decide to confront your friend about his storytelling. Gradually, you start to express your concerns and hope that the friendship can be saved.

What would be an ideal title for this passage?

- No more liars
- Different story each day
- Building trust in friendships.

What is the main idea of the passage?

- Friends who are liars need an audience with active listening skills.
- Good and solid friendships should be established through honesty.
- Good relationships consist of untruths.

Activity 9.4 Discussion question

How would you approach this problem using critical thinking if you had to explain this scenario in the discussions?

Critical thinking and essay development

Critical thinking in essay development often requires reading and time to research possible material to support your views, as explained in Chapter 3. Research is needed in order for you to form an opinion, decide if the sources are reliable, fact-check information, and express yourself clearly in writing. Critical thinking is needed in order to decide on what issues you will address in the paper, decide on the analysis and claims that you will make and need to support in the paper, and evaluate any learning outcomes that you want to occur as a result of your paper and research. Essays should produce some type of learning for you as the student and hopefully introduce concepts and highlight what you know and have learned. Critical thinking should be part of this discovery process.

Activity 9.5 Persuasive short argument

Write a persuasive short argument for or against a controversial topic. Your argument should be no more than two pages with citations to support your viewpoints.

Activity 9.6 Critical thinking short review

You reviewed critical thinking while using the Internet, completing discussion questions, performing time management, and writing essays. Select one and share what you learned in 150 to 200 words.

Critical thinking and ethics

Critical thinking often involves evaluating and analyzing situations to find the best possible solution for the situation, as explained in Chapter 3. Your ethics illustrate your reasons or deliver a position for a moral decision or perspective. If your personal ethics can answer some of your questions, such as whether this is the right decision for you or whether this is morally acceptable, then applying critical thinking becomes an easier part of the thinking process. Your ethical views will help you when applying critical thinking to situations. In essence, your ethical principles usually guide your decisions. The final product of your critical thinking should result in some type of logic and morality if you are making ethical decisions.

It was explained in Chapter 3 that the assumptions and inferences that you make can influence critical thinking. "An assumption is something we take for granted or presuppose" (Paul and Elder, 2006).[1] For example, if you learned from your friends that computers are difficult to learn, you might assume this to be true before actually working with them. This is an assumption. "Inference is a step of the mind, an intellectual act by which one concludes that something is true in light of something else's being true or seeming to be true" (Paul and Elder, 2006). For example, your friend has a computer in his office. You can infer that he is computer literate; that seems to be true since he has the computer.

How do assumptions and inferences relate to ethics and critical thinking? Think about this for a moment. If you have made assumptions and inferences based on incomplete information or what is supposed to be true, that will impact the way you apply a thinking process. You might make decisions and not understand all the facts regarding the situation because you have false information. Your ethics could be compromised because you are basing your views on biases and stereotypes as opposed to examining the situation for the truth.

Paul and Elder (2006) explained that when individuals do not exercise critical thinking, they might not be aware of the needs of others. They might focus on their personal needs as opposed to the viewpoints of others and how incorrect their views are regarding a situation. Critical thinkers should implement the following to be fair-minded in their thinking:

- Analyze the logic of situations and problems.
- Ask clear and precise questions.
- Check information for accuracy and relevance.

- Distinguish between raw information and someone's interpretation of it.

- Recognize assumptions guiding inferences.

- Identify prejudicial and biased beliefs, unjustifiable conclusions, misused words, and missed implications.

- Notice when one's viewpoint is biased by selfish interest.

Students must make ethical choices that involve critical thinking with regard to school work and planning to complete assignments. Unethical choices made by students who fail to use logic or morality can easily result in immoral behaviours in class. Could it also possibly be that the practice of poor ethics in the classroom, such as cheating, can transfer into the workforce? It is not a win-win situation. Working simply to meet the goals, and not doing the work or putting in the effort to learn and embrace the college time, is not making the most out of the learning opportunity. It is not applying critical thinking to the work and it is not making ethical choices.

Often, when thinking about critical thinking and ethics, it is visceral to believe that people with good ethics exercise critical thinking. It is also visceral to think that ethics are sometimes compromised as a result of success. How do critical thinking and ethics connect? Participate in the activity below for insight.

Activity 9.7 Ethics and critical thinking responses

Review the following comments from students. Respond with a rebuttal or counterpoint as to why you agree or disagree with the statements regarding ethics and critical thinking:

1. Students must make ethical decisions in an online classroom because unethical behaviour there is harder to monitor than on campus. Trusting students makes online classes possible.

2. Critical thinking can define ethics. In the workforce, there are many unethical decisions made every day. Unethical decisions often hurt the minority parties involved.

3. Personally, I do not think ethics can exist without critical thinking. To act in an ethical manner or make an ethical decision, it takes a thought process especially for the person to know his or her truth, evaluate the situation, and make a decision.

4. Critical thinking is the process of analyzing information to come to a decision. It weighs the possible outcomes and consequences of one's actions. This is where ethics plays a part in critical thinking. If a person is morally responsible, his or her decisions usually reflect personal ethics.

5. Critical thinking can be used in one form or another when making ethical decisions. As a general rule, critical thinking requires developing some emotional and intellectual distance between you and your ideas. It is not an emotional decision.

6. Our pursuit of having more and doing better can cloud our judgment, allowing us to set aside our ethics and values. Critical thinking has no place in ethics.

7. In my opinion, ethics play a major role in critical thinking. For every situation you may be faced with, you should apply critical thinking to ensure the most positive outcome.

8. Ethics are related to critical thinking because moral principles should guide our problem solving and decision

making. The results of our critical thinking should be logical *and* moral. Unethical ideas that *seem* logical fail to recognize the full impact of immoral choices.

Let us connect the aspects discussed about critical thinking in the decision-making process throughout this course. Review *Smith's critical thinking circle*™ in Figure 9.1. Reflect on the decision to return to school that a student follows in the critical thinking process.

External and internal factors have a significant role in critical thinking and making informed decisions.

Figure 9.1   Smith's critical thinking circle™

In the middle of the *critical thinking circle* is the issue that needs critical thinking applied to it. In this scenario, the issue to be addressed is the student returning to school and enrolling in online classes. The thinking process penetrates throughout the circle based on the issue.

Internal factors

Close to the middle of the thinking process inside the circle are internal factors. Internal factors consist of your thoughts about the issue, whether they are logical or illogical thoughts. They are close to the root of the issue in the center of the circle. They include your emotional feelings or fears that are prompting your thoughts from past experiences such as divorce, work relationships, death, health issues, school concerns, and inner thoughts regarding what family and friends have commented. Some examples of thoughts about returning to school could be feelings of inadequacies, time commitment concerns, school choices, and personal problems that could conflict with school based on any past experiences.

Or, thoughts could be simple reflections of what has occurred in your life that could have an impact on your choices. Internal factors could consist of your reflections of ethical choices or lack of ethical choices regarding the issue. Perhaps you were in school for some time and did not take it seriously. Your life was about parties, dating, and having a social life more than the attention required for academic studies. As your thoughts become more detailed and internally reflective, you go further in the internal critical thinking circle. You begin to pose questions to yourself in this stage about the issue and possible answers in the inner part of the circle. What if distance education classes are challenging and I cannot keep up due to lack of computer skills? How will I submit my work to the instructor? Do I have to log in at the same time? How does it work? Why is this school a better choice for me over another? You assess any answers to the questions that you have posed such as the following. Distance education degrees – are they credible? I have heard that most of the teachers are part-time and are really not active in the classroom. What if my teacher is inactive? You have projected outcomes. For example, if I get sick and cannot finish my degree then I will not be able to complete my degree. If the course is difficult then I will not be able to follow along in class. Or, I can finally search for another career or be an entrepreneur if I graduate from college. I am guaranteed to make more money than I make now. I do not have to log in at set times, only meet my assignment deadlines at this school, which is preferable. New ideas are often formed in this stage and the ideas formed can increase internal confidence levels, resulting in desired outcomes. New ideas could consist of having the confidence to solve the problem and then taking the action steps to enroll in school or define the best possible solution for your issue. The internal factors influencing thought processes extend through the circle.

External factors

The external factors are located on the outside lines of the circle (revisit Figure 9.1). External factors are influential in the critical thinking process because influences are coming from exterior factors to which you assign meaning, such as family or friends' comments or opinions, based on whether you accept or reject the information. "You are too old to return to school." "You weren't focused the first time so what is different now?" "I think that you will do great returning to school, and I am behind you 100 percent."

"Can you really attend classes online and receive a valid degree? That cannot be possible!"

External factors could include social media and literature regarding the issue. What do reading materials and social website testimonials say about older adults returning to school? Can adults meet their goals when learning from a distance? External factors could impact thought processes as you progress with critical thinking, deciding on what to do. You start to engage in more assumptions and inferences and this time with the help or hindrances from literature, social websites, and family or friends who are not really involved in the matter but are in some form information carriers. Or, the carriers of information could be speaking from their experiences and offering answers to any questions that you pose to them in this stage as well as opinions. You might gather opinions from others from questions posed, such as the following. What if the statistics are correct? Do you know anyone who attended online classes? What if I won't be able to understand in online classes because the teacher is not present? How well do you perform in online instruction? Then, you might reject some of the statements that you gathered from others and pose more positive questions to yourself such as "What if I can meet my goals and the course material is not difficult to learn?" You might reason in your critical thinking process that after all, you do have life experiences, and you are capable.

In addition, your outcomes of past experiences from relationships and ethical or unethical choices are also part of this external area because these outcomes have more than likely resulted from external factors as opposed to projected outcomes from internal factors. The external factors influencing thought processes extend through the circle as well. Hopefully, new ideas are developed throughout this thinking process to help you make a great, ethical decision.

Internal and external factors can influence the critical thinking process. If you analyze the circle, you can probably determine that there are lots of pieces of information, experiences, and opinions from others that could influence critical thinking and the decision-making process on any topic to which you need to apply critical thinking. It is important to be able to distinguish between fact and opinion, bias and truth, emotion and logic in order to make a decision. Ideally, a critical thinking process consists of internal and external factors that produce new insights and perspectives in order to be comfortable with a decision that is personally acceptable. It is thinking at its best without confusion. If confusion is involved in the process, you might want to rethink the external and internal factors that could be resonating louder in your mental thought process than the logical facts.

Summary

In order to make good decisions and illustrate ethical behaviours, self-critique and self-reflection are needed in the critical thinking process. This is a personal journey. A journey in which you can ask yourself questions about who you are, why you behave a certain way, what you have to prove – why you feel that you need to prove this, what does a good or poor choice consist of, and why good or bad. There are numerous questions that can be asked to examine your ways of behaviour and result in applying critical thinking to help you make ethical choices. Critical thinking should be applied to time management and your assignments so that the high level of thinking is represented in your work. Internal and external factors can influence the decisions that you make when you are processing information. Examining these factors can help you get to the root cause

---

What would you do?

A student once asked whether purchasing a paper off the Internet and placing the website where she retrieved the information in the paper is considered plagiarism. Do you think that critical thinking was exercised in this scenario?

Figure 9.2　Self-reflection

of ethical or unethical behaviour and that can help you isolate unnecessary factors to make personal quality decisions.

Note

1.　Paul, R. and Elder, L. *Critical Thinking: Tools for Taking Charge of Your Learning and Your Life, 2nd,* © 2006. Printed and electronically reproduced by permission of Pearson Education, Inc., Upper Saddle River, New Jersey.

10

Ethical expectations: students

Abstract: A clear indicator that the adult student is committed to a degree is when the student has a clear vision of his or her goals and has identified specific values. Success and values are measured differently. For the ethical student, following what is presently the acceptable protocol and procedures is morally apparent. In addition, the ethical student is learning with a purpose, not simply learning the content to pass the course. The final chapter provides diverse student perspectives about success and values. Students review information on motivation and learning with a purpose. Scenarios where choices were made that did not highlight a commitment to class will be exemplified along with reflective activities. This chapter concludes with a list of ethical behavioural patterns in the online environment that could help ensure students' success rates.

Key words: goals, values, ethical patterns.

Ethical expectations

If critical thinking requires posing questions to yourself, such as when, where, why, and how, then your ethics can be part of the answers – the solutions to your critical thinking. It helps to apply critical thinking when making ethical decisions. This applies to meeting *goals* as the adult learner. You must decide on the importance of your goals and how committed you will be to meeting those goals. What are your expectations for school? If you are in school for a degree then it should be your mission to do the work and avoid the repercussions for not doing the work. Remember, everything is a choice and everything has a consequence.

Having a clear picture of your goals can help you reach them. Write your daily, weekly, or monthly goals. Track milestones and be mindful of the process that allows you to reach the milestone, such as composing a business plan for a business goal or saving money to purchase school books. The small, action-oriented steps help reach milestones to bring the goal into fruition.

Be sure that your goals are *value* based. Values are personal beliefs. They are what you deem as important for your life and what you adhere to as you meet your goals. Some people value health, happiness, success, wealth, and family. What are your values? If you value a good education, then your goal for obtaining your degree is based on that value. You will do the work honestly and uphold the integrity of your work.

Success can often be a value. Success is defined differently for each individual. For some people, success could mean being wealthy. For others, success can mean being wealthy and intellectual. How do you define success? Hopefully, there is a balance of hard work, commitment, and honesty in your success definition.

Activity 10.1 Values and success scenarios

Can a person with no values be successful? Read the following comments. Respond with a rebuttal or counterpoint as to why you agree or disagree with the statements regarding success and values.

1. Success can be measured in many ways. It varies, depending on what success means to an individual person. I measure personal success in both small and large increments of self-triumph.

2. Many times, success is measured by how much you can cast aside values, convictions or even sincerity.

3. I, personally, measure success in a business aspect. In business, everyone remembers your failures. However, when you succeed in business, it is remembered for a short time, and then the bar is set for your next success.

4. Often, in the eyes of the people who are performing the unethical practices, they tend to see absolutely nothing wrong with what they are doing and see the benefits as a personal achievement (success) or something that is owed to them.

5. I believe that people with no values, convictions and/or sincerity towards others may be successful, but I believe that it depends on their line of work and that their percentage of success will probably be lower because of these issues and the success can be short term.

Activity 10.2 Discussion questions

What are your values? Have you noticed a change in them in the last five years? What might have shifted in your perspective to make a difference in what you value?

What are your goals? Have you assessed them and identified how to track them and meet certain milestones? What are your thoughts regarding goal setting?

Learning with a purpose

Learning with a purpose means to learn to apply the information that is being processed and to have a knowledge base and develop intellect. Learning with a purpose does not include learning the material simply to pass a test. That would include only committing information to short-term memory. "Short-term memory refers to information that is mentally processed in the brain that is temporary" (Plotnik, 2005).[1] Paying attention commits information into short-term memory but, after a short time, information fades unless it is rehearsed. Some information is eventually stored to permanent memory. As a learner, it is important to rehearse what you are learning so that more information can be stored to permanent memory, known as long-term memory. "Long-term memory refers to the process of storing almost unlimited amounts of information over long periods of time with the potential of retrieving or remembering the information for immediate or future knowledge" (Plotnik, 2005).[1] This information is usually meaningful and relevant. It requires elaborative rehearsal. "Elaborative rehearsal involves using effort to actively make meaningful associations between new information that you wish to remember and old or familiar information that is already stored in long-term memory" (Plotnik, 2005).[1] For example, if you were trying to remember an important concept learned in one of your classes, you might try to associate the concept with sensory details, such as any feelings or memories about the concept. You might try to compare the concept to a current event. This is elaborative rehearsal because you are calling to mind associations in order to commit the information to long-term memory.

Activity 10.3 Discussion questions

Recall how you can use elaborative rehearsal to learn effective research online. How has this aided you to learn with a purpose and use critical thinking to approach research?

Why is it important to try to commit information to long-term memory? How can this be helpful with regard to you learning with a purpose?

In some of the examples presented in this book, some adult learners were not learning with a purpose. They wanted the easy way out of doing the work. College is an exploratory time in the learning process. College is a privilege. It is counterproductive to not do the work.

Compulsion to do badly

Are you a person who exemplifies a radical type of behaviour? If so, do you have to change? Are you the type of person who loves a good debate? Does this means that there is something wrong with your behaviour? Is change necessary to meet your degree goals? We have established that right behaviour is not necessarily right for everyone in Chapter 2, when the ethical theories were introduced. So, it might be safe to use the word acceptable behaviour. As an adult learner, you do not have to change who you are and are not forced to change, but you must follow the rules and adapt if you want meet your college goals.

The beauty of online learning is that diverse groups of individuals come together to experience shared learning from one another. You will meet people who are heavily radical, argumentative, intuitive, supportive, sensitive, comical, and any adjective that you could guess and that is what makes the online learning experience unlimited. You will learn from your peers and even through conflict resolution. You might also discover that even though you do not have to change, you adapt to the rules to meet your goals and conform to the order of the classroom. You might find that in the adaptation, a new mindset is produced that causes you to change simply on your own – to want to change – or new perspectives cause you not to be as radical in class or in professional settings.

Commitment to class

Learning with a purpose requires commitment to class work. What does it mean to make a commitment to doing your own work online? Read the following scenarios and reflect on commitment to class.

Scenario one

"I will be attending military training for the next two weeks. I will try very hard to participate as much as I can, and still get my assignments in on time. Please forgive me in my absence."

Scenario two

"Hello. I just wanted to let you know I have been falling behind on some assignments due to being married this past Saturday. This week's assignments/discussions that were due Friday are now being turned in today, Sunday. I missed last week's assignments due to finalizing the wedding plans. I hope to receive full credit for this week's assignment submitted today."

Scenario three

"My computer crashed and I had car trouble this week. I was not able to submit my work but will submit soon."

As an online student (and some adult learners are aware of this and comply), it is your responsibility to submit work, as explained in Chapter 5 regarding moral dilemmas and online excuses. Think about these scenarios for another second. If you were in a traditional classroom, that is a face-to-face college, would you inform your instructor that you cannot submit work because you were married last week, but you are going to submit it now? There are certain liberties that online students take that are not necessarily displayed in face-to-face academic settings. Some students in a traditional college usually accept the responsibility for their work if it is missed, without the excuses or rationale that some online students present. Sometimes students in a traditional college will explain extenuating events that have led to missed work, such as the loss of a loved one. Usually, the school has a policy in place for missed work. The daily occurrences that some online students wish to disclose for courses that are usually five to ten weeks at the most are unnecessary. It is important as the adult learner to submit your work and adhere to the school's late policy in the event that you cannot submit work. The instructor does not need to be informed about your daily hassles.

There should not be constant excuses provided in emails about class work. It is wise to consider having a backup plan for technical issues. Simply because you are enrolled in an online class and have computer issues, this does not pardon work being missed. There will be technology issues and that is inevitable. Commitment to class work is your ethical responsibility if you want to meet your degree goals; it is the acceptable choice.

Activity 10.4 Discussion questions

Do you believe that there are certain liberties that accompany online education in communication? What are your thoughts about liberties online? Do you think that students are free to type what they want because they are not face to face, but rather in an electronic environment? What is the significance of your relationship to the person reading your message online as opposed to face to face? Should there be a difference in communication methods?

Activity 10.5 PC behaviour

Read the scenario in Figure 10.1 and explain your views on the students' response.

Ethics are a concern in an academic environment because people always want to make sure that they are being treated fairly. Colleges and universities have been places where students are taught to speak their minds and feel free to be expressive about themselves and their behaviours. But what happens when students or faculty object to certain comments, saying that they are offended by them? That question is at the heart of an ongoing discussion called PC behaviour. PC is a term which supposedly restricts actions and speech that are viewed as offensive or harmful to some groups, such as minorities and people with disabilities. Some schools have issued punishments for those who promote such negative behaviours. It is a good idea to have some form of behaviour management in place to remind people that they cannot just say what they want, simply because they are online. Respect is still a requirement!

Figure 10.1 PC behaviour

Activity 10.6 Discussion questions

What does it mean to be committed to class work? Why is it important to be mindful that online communication should illustrate a level of respect in messages?

Ethical disposition

Along with a commitment to classes and learning with a purpose, you must decide on your ethical disposition to be successful as an online student. Ethical disposition means your viewpoint on the issue or outlook on life. Do you remember the child scenario from Chapter 1? He might have been raised in a home where he learned right from wrong, but he still had a choice as an adult learner – so do you. What is your ethical disposition? What are your perspectives regarding your choices and how they impact others? If you are the type of person who naturally tries to display humanistic characteristics and live as your best self, then your ethical disposition will not be influenced by inadequate decisions or challenges. You will probably remain consistent and stable in your viewpoints and actions to reach your goals. If you are the type of person who wavers in your ethical disposition and can be influenced by events not going your way and wanting to alter the outcomes, be aware that you could jeopardize your ethical disposition. Are you the type of person who exhibits extreme behaviour? Do you go from one extreme to another?

There has to be a level of responsibility that you take as an adult student. Read the case of Alex in Figure 10.2. The instructor accepted his late work without penalty but he did not receive full points due to grammatical errors, and not because the assignment was late. Some instructors will try to work with students in spite of the late policy. He was angry and rude in the first email after receiving the courtesy of having late work accepted. He submitted his responses late for a second week and the instructor informed him that she could not accept his work. The dialogue begins during the second week of class.

Alex

Instructor Realms,

I cannot believe that you took points off my work. I thought I had submitted my work on time last week. I am questioning your grading. I dislike teachers like you who are not consistent. Also, why did I receive point deductions this week?

Instructor Realms

Hi Alex,

I accepted late work from you last week as a courtesy and deducted points for grammar, not because your work was late. This week, I had to apply late points. I have to be fair to all students. Be sure that your work is in class. It is your responsibility to double-check. The late policy is in the syllabus located in the course expectations folder in class. You can also go through the grade appeal process with your advisor if you disagree. I addressed this with you last week, as well as your behaviour. Please be sure to review the netiquette rules in the syllabus as well.

Alex

I was just letting you know, and I am ahead of you. I have spoken with my advisor about your teaching style. As for my behaviour, you are not my parents, so you didn't address anything with me. I cannot wait until this class ends because you seriously irritate me.

Figure 10.2 Student case Alex

Activity 10.7 Discussion questions

What do you think about this scenario? Would you be reluctant to address an instructor face to face in the style described above, with students taking certain liberties online for granted? What is wrong with this behaviour from an adult learner? What is your ethnical disposition regarding being an online student? What do you deem as important about being an ethical online student?

You also should avoid placing your instructor in unethical positions by simply making certain statements. Read the case of Deb in Figure 10.3 addressing an instructor and record your thoughts.

I followed your instructions as best as I could to understand this assignment. According to some of the other classmates, they also find the assignment confusing. I just want you to know that this is my final class, and I cannot afford to get less than a "C." So I'm asking that you consider the complications of this assignment because it may not come across as comprehensive for some students. Please consider this when grading my assignment this week. Thanks. Deb.

Figure 10.3   Student case Deb

What do you think about this scenario?

Motivation

Motivation is a key factor in determining if an online student will be successful. It can make the difference in completing class assignments or participating in class. When you are motivated as a student, you want to meet your goals, regardless of how you are feeling. Realistically, energy levels are not high every day. Some days are stressful for adult learners. These are the days when motivation is of the essence.

Transformational experiences

Transformational experiences can cause adults to learn and seek ways to learn and they serve as motivators. Transformational experiences can result in an adult learner having a new perspective, and they are not always easy or unchallenging experiences. For some adult learners, a divorce can be a transformational experience. This can cause them to seek new ways of learning and new experiences. Returning to college could be one of these experiences. The transformational experiences and remembrance of the experiences can serve as motivation to achieve a higher goal.

When certain needs are met for the adult learner, the adult is motivated by new perspectives learned in class. The reward of meeting a degree goal is driven by the self-empowerment and confidence of the goal and the journey. These serve as motivation when the adult struggles to remain motivated. The transformational experiences cause changes in individuals and how they might perceive the world around them.

Activity 10.8 Transformational experiences

Review the transformational experience in Figure 10.4. How do you think transformational experiences are helping the learner, if at all? What do you notice about this student's response that is impacting school work? Should the teacher be sympathetic? After all, a loss has occurred.

Hello Instructor

I just got off the phone with Cindy, the academic advisor, and she informed me that I need to pass this course with a C. I was wondering whether if I was to do my assignments that I did not complete, would I be able to get credit minus some points? In addition, my backpack with my books and my laptop were stolen from me while I was sleeping at a park. And this year marks the anniversary of my mother's death. That is why my assignments were not complete. Through all the changes and negative possibilities, I still returned to school, and I am committed to my degree. I am going to attempt to pass and give it my all as I previously stated. I am sorry for any inconvenience this may have caused.

Figure 10.4   **Transformational experiences**

Activity 10.9 Discussion questions

Have you experienced any transformational experiences that have led to your return to school? Did you gain or have you gained new perspectives since being enrolled in school, and released some old ways of thinking?

Activity 10.10 Questions to consider

Here are some questions to consider as you end this course:

- Who do you want to be in the classroom?
- What is your character online?
- Is it acceptable to make up stories to fulfill discussion question requirements?
- Do you evade the truth in order to submit a response?
- Have you formulated a plan to work smart in college?

- Do you have a backup plan for computer problems while attending school online?

- Do you have popular educational websites to visit for scholarly sources bookmarked on your Internet browser?

- Have you assessed your writing abilities?

- What are your thoughts about plagiarizing? How do you plan to avoid plagiarism?

- What do you value about online learning and obtaining your degree?

Your instructor might ask you to respond to one or more of these questions in detail.

Tips for being a successful online student

There are *ten ethical patterns* that online students should implement to be successful. They are the alternative choices to poor behaviour. They are the good (acceptable) choices to ensure your success as a college student. At this point, you have reviewed how ethical decisions can influence your success. You have also reviewed how critical thinking should be exercised when completing class work and allocating time for class work on your college journey. Here are more tips that are important to implement as an online student:

1. *Allocate time* for reading class content, textbook material, and assignments. – reading is the number one strategy that you can implement for yourself as an online student.

2. *Check in* regularly – if you attend classes online, check in to class regularly and check for emails from instructors,

even if you have met attendance and assignment requirements. If you do not, you can miss an important message about your assignment that could impact your grade.

3. *Proofread* your work – be confident in what you submit. If you are not happy with the presentation and content of the work, do not submit it. Your work represents you.

4. *Avoid* the excuses – remember that you have a goal to meet, so do the work.

5. *Assert* positive energy – even if you have experienced some challenges, the online classroom and being in school are positive attributes for your journey.

6. *Get* self-awareness and define your truth.

7. *Form* your own opinions – you do have them.

8. *Document* all work that is not yours.

9. *Become* a self-directed learner and basically seek to learn.

10. *Do* the hard work – remember to be an independent thinker and that you have ideas.

Activity 10.11 Ethical patterns

Select two ethical patterns from the list and explain why they are important to you as an adult, online student.

Summary

Meeting goals, learning with a purpose, and being committed to class are all steps in the right direction to being a successful online student. Assessing your choices and reasons for exhibiting unacceptable behaviour can provide the results that you need to make better choices if you allow change or accept that change is needed. Following the *ten ethical patterns* and staying motivated can also ensure that you meet school goals without the ramifications of unethical decisions. This is your time to learn and illustrate your knowledge. Implementing the necessary ethical steps will help you advance throughout your college tenure without significant problems in the online environment.

Closing remarks

Ultimately, there are two paths to explore in life when meeting a goal, as the notable Robert Frost explained in his poem *The Road Not Taken*, and they are the path most explored and the path least explored. The paths easily diverge but they have a common starting point and that is meeting a specific goal, the college degree goal. The path most explored is full of familiarity. Others have explored the same path. Sometimes the path most explored is easy and involves fewer obstacles than the path least explored. The path most explored is full of open doors and some enter every door for quick success. The path least explored is the one that allows individual expression. It is the path that involves self-assessment to meet goals. It is the path where sacrifices and obstacles are often high in number. It is the path that bypasses certain fast doors to enjoy the journey and build a future with longevity in the distance. It is a good choice to choose the latter. Do the hard work to meet your goals. Become a self-directed, ethical learner. Learn like you never learned before as an adult learner. Remember, education implodes the walls of ignorance.

What would you do?

Will you do the hard work to meet your goals, learn, and not take any shortcuts? Will you exhibit ethical behaviour online?

Figure 10.5 Self-reflection

Note

1. Plotnik, R. *Introduction to Psychology (with InfoTrac®)*, 7E. © 2005 Wadsworth, a part of Cengage Learning, Inc. Reproduced by permission *www.cengage.com/permissions*.

References

Anderson, L.W., Krathwohl, D.R., Airasian, P.W., Cruikshank, K.A., Mayer, R.E et al. (2001). *A Taxonomy for Learning, Teaching and Assessing: A Revision of Bloom's Taxonomy of Educational Objectives*, abridged edn. Upper Saddle River, NJ: Pearson Education, Inc.

Brookfield, S.D. (1987). *Developing Critical Thinkers: Challenging Adults to Explore Alternative ways of Thinking and Acting.* San Francisco: Jossey-Bass.

Brookfield, S.D. (1995). *Becoming a Critically Reflective Teacher.* San Francisco: Jossey-Bass.

Grammar Girl. Available at: *http://grammar.quickanddirty tips.com/* (accessed 8 August 2011).

Lake, J. (2011). The shifting nature of plagiarism and the challenge to international foundation courses. *In-Form*, 1: 12–13. University of London International Studies. Available at: *http://www.soas.ac.uk/staff/staff31292.php* (accessed 4 August 2011).

Merriam, S.B., Caffarella, R.S. and Baumgartner, L.M. (2007). *Learning in Adulthood. A Comprehensive Guide.* San Francisco: Jossey-Bass.

Myers-Briggs Type Indicator® (MBTI®). Available at: *http:// www.myersbriggs.org/my-mbti-personality-type/mbti-basics/* (accessed 5 July 2011).

Panza, C. and Potthast, A. (2010). *Ethics for Dummies.* Hoboken, NJ: Wiley Publishing.

Paul, R. and Elder, L. (2006). *Critical Thinking: Tools for Taking Charge of Your Learning and Your Life*, Upper Saddle River, NJ: Pearson Education, Inc.

Plotnik, R. (2005) *Introduction to Psychology.* Belmont, CA: Wadsworth.

Purdue. Available at: *http://owl.english.purdue.edu/* (accessed 8 August 2011).

Sutherland-Smith, W. Deakin University, Australia. Available at: *http://www.deakin.edu.au/itl/contact/profiles/wendy-ss.php* (accessed 27 July 2011).

Thomas, K.W. and Kilmann, R.H. (1974, 2002, 2007). *Thomas–Kilmann Conflict Mode Instrument.* CPP, Inc. Available at: *https://www.cpp.com/products/tki/tki_info. aspx* (accessed 5 July 2011).

Ültanır, G.Y. and Ültanır, E. (2010). Exploring the Curriculum Dimensions of Theories-Based Adult Education – A Sample Course of Southeast Antatolian Region. *International Journal of Instruction*, 3(2): 4–23.

Index

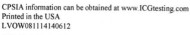

CPSIA information can be obtained at www.ICGtesting.com
Printed in the USA
LVOW081114140612

286016LV00001B/1/P

9 781843 346890